*TUNEUPS: When are they necessary?

*BELTS, CHAINS, HOSES: What are they—
and what do they do?

*HEATING AND COOLING SYSTEMS:
What kinds of problems can you expect—and
what can you do about them?

*POOR MILEAGE: What could be causing it?

Even if you don't know a diesel engine from a
distributor cap, you can find out how to give
your car the tender loving care it needs . . .
and, in many cases, solve problems on the
spot. This illustrated troubleshooting guide can
help you cut down on car trouble and
expensive repair bills—for smoother, safer,
stress-free rides.

**KEEP THIS BOOK IN YOUR
GLOVE COMPARTMENT**

# KEEP THIS BOOK IN YOUR GLOVE COMPARTMENT

By
**"Motorman" Leon Kaplan**

BERKLEY BOOKS, NEW YORK

KEEP THIS BOOK IN YOUR GLOVE COMPARTMENT

A Berkley Book / published by arrangement with
the author

PRINTING HISTORY
Berkley edition / October 1997

The Penguin Putnam Inc. World Wide Web site address is
http://www.penguinputnam.com

ISBN: 0-425-15020-8

BERKLEY®
Berkley Books are published by The Berkley Publishing Group,
a member of Penguin Putnam Inc.,
375 Hudson Street, New York, New York 10014.
BERKLEY and the "B" design
are trademarks belonging to Berkley Publishing Corporation.

PRINTED IN THE UNITED STATES OF AMERICA

10   9   8   7   6   5   4   3

# WARNINGS AND CAUTIONS

Due to the complex nature of the motor vehicle, it is very important that you always exercise the utmost care when working on your vehicle. Before attempting any service or repair, always consult your owner's manual and, preferably, an approved shop repair manual for your particular vehicle. These manuals will point out specific repair procedures and, more importantly, personal safety precautions. If you are in the least bit confused about any particular procedure, consult a professional technician. Remember to always wear eye protection and, if necessary, hand protection.

# TABLE OF CONTENTS

# ACKNOWLEDGMENTS

I would like to thank the people whose confidence and encouragement was so important to me in pursuing my hobby (working with motors/engines) and turning that interest into a satisfying career: my parents Ava and Oscar Kaplan, my brothers Ben, Edward and Robert, and my grandparents Helen and Edward Lance.

My wife Eileene (a.k.a. "Dixie Bell"), along with my children Jeff, Jill, and Lance had to put up with my long hours at the shop and an entertainment career that has kept me away from home many weekdays and weekends.

For my formal training, I have the highest regard for the Nashville Auto/Diesel College in Tennessee. I'm much obliged to president and founder Thomas Balls for the creation of such a fine institution.

The organizing of this material was accomplished by Gil Cormaci, marketing/public relations consultant and my close friend.

Technical support and artwork was supplied by the following companies and associations:

AlliedSignal, Inc.—FRAM Filters, Autolite Spark Plugs, Bendix Brake Products
Car Care Council
Cooper Automotive—Champion Spark Plugs, Wagner Lighting, Power Path Wire and Cable
DANA Corporation—Perfect Circle
Gates Rubber Company—Gates Belts and Hoses
Goodyear Tire & Rubber Company—Goodyear Tires, Goodyear Belts and Hoses
Meguiar's Inc.
Monroe Auto Equipment—Monroe Shocks and Struts

Moog Automotive
Wagner Brake Products
Valvoline Motor Oil

    Grandma Lance told me something when I was young that has always stayed with me and has served as inspiration: "The only time Success comes before Work is in the dictionary." Thank you, everyone.

                                         L.K.

# PREFACE

The purchase of an automobile is typically the second biggest investment you'll make, next to your house. My advice for you is to take good care of this investment.

This book is intended to help you ensure that your vehicle has a long life, performs at peak efficiency, and returns to you the lowest cost-per-mile operating expense and safety on the road.

You'll learn about the many components of the automobile—from under the hood to under the car. You'll be able to diagnose problems and know when to attempt the repair yourself and when to seek the help of a professional technician.

There have been many advances in automotive technology during the past few years. In most cases, it's not a matter of simply changing plugs, points and condenser, etc. Most vehicles today are governed by a sophisticated onboard computer system. You'd be surprised by the number of callers to my weekly radio show and letters from folks who have been told they have a "computer problem." Sound familiar? The following pages will help you to understand what's going on when you get that kind of response from your technician.

I've serviced automobiles for more than forty years, and I've encountered just about every conceivable automotive problem.

My fascination with motors and engines began during my youth in Durham, North Carolina, following World War II. It seems that if it was motorized, I had to tinker with it. And, it all started with the family lawnmower, to which I added dual exhaust. It sure helped me get through the yard chores a lot quicker.

I also was aware of the gas-powered washing machine; however, I couldn't figure out a way to hot rod it to get through the laundry quicker.

My first business venture, at the age of twelve, was with bicycles. A company called Wizzer had a motor kit for bicycles, so I became the "converter" in town. Wizzer engines were the first I actually took apart and reassembled. Such a simple design (I'm fortunate to own two Wizzers currently). Remember them?

Like a lot of you who grew up on a farm, I had my first experience behind the wheel with a tractor. I would gladly spread manure all day for nothing just to be able to drive.

And today, because of the nature of my business, I drive more different cars in one month than most people drive in a lifetime. Based on my experience, I believe that if you follow my tips you'll save money and feel safer behind the wheel because you'll become your car's best technician.

So keep this guide handy—in your glove compartment or somewhere nearby. Use it and enjoy many hours of . . . Happy Motoring!

Leon Kaplan

## IMPORTANT NUMBERS
## FOR INSTANT REFERENCE

Your License Plate Number_____

Your Vehicle Serial Number (VIN)_____

Vehicle Year____Make_____ Model Number_____

Tire Size_____Tire Pressure: Front_____Rear_____

Brand of Tires_____

Oil Capacity_____Oil Filter Part Number_____

Air Filter Part Number_____Spark Plug Type_____

Battery Type_____

Date of Purchase of Vehicle_____

Name of Dealer (or Individual)_____

Address_____

City_____State_____Zip_____

Telephone (___)_____

Length of Factory Warranty: Drivetrain_____

Length of Factory Warranty: Rest of Vehicle_____

Any Other Warranty (Type and Length)_____

Name of Auto Insurance Carrier_____

Agent's Name_____

Carrier's Address_____

City_____State_____Zip_____

Telephone_____

Policy Number_____

Expiration Date of Policy_____

# WHAT SHOULD YOU CARRY WITH YOU AT ALL TIMES WHEN MOTORING

- Flashlight and extra batteries
- Emergency flashers
- Fire extinguisher
- Work gloves
- Small set of tools
- Quart of motor oil
- 2 one-gallon containers of water
- Tire pressure gauge
- Duct tape
- Battery jumper cables
- Radio with extra batteries
- Small change for phone calls or tolls
- Window cleaner and rags
- *Personal items:* Sunglasses, tissue, moist towlettes, pair of walking shoes, sweater or jacket, "Space" blanket.

# WHAT TO DO AFTER AN ACCIDENT

The Automotive Service Association (ASA), a nonprofit trade association serving the automotive service industry, recommends that you take the following steps after an accident to decrease your chance of complications later on:

1. Move your vehicle to a safe place, and stop and identify yourself to the other driver. If your vehicle cannot be moved, turn on the hazard lights. Proceed carefully to determine if there are injuries, and seek medical help if needed. Notify the police and tell them who you are and where you are, and relate the details of the accident. Let them know of any injuries or if anyone claims to be injured.

2. Exchange information with the other vehicle driver, including driver's license number and vehicle registration number. It's also a good idea to take down the vehicle make, model, and license plate number. Make sure to get the other driver's name, address, telephone number, and the name of their insurance company. Also make a list of the names and addresses of any passengers and witnesses.

3. Make sure to get the names and badge numbers of any police officers who arrive at the scene of the accident. Police officers will file a report on your accident if there are injuries. If a report is filed, ask how to obtain a copy of it at a later date.

4. At the scene of the accident, avoid any extensive discussions about who was responsible for the damage. If the other person admits responsibility, offers a monetary settlement, and you accept, then your right to file a claim against the driver may be compromised. Also, never agree to just forget about the accident. Even though there are no visible signs of damage to your vehicle, you may find that there is hidden structural damage. The same is true for bodily injuries that may not be reported until a few days after the accident.

5. Write a complete description of the accident as soon as possible. Your description should include weather conditions, estimated speeds, time of day, road conditions, and the direction in which you and the other vehicle were traveling at the time of the accident. Draw a rough sketch of the site of the accident, and make notes about any statements made by the driver or witnesses. If you happen to be traveling with a camera at the time of your accident, take photos of the damaged vehicles and the accident site.

6. Have the vehicle towed or driven to the collision repair facility of your choice.

7. Notify your insurance company of the accident as soon as possible.

Documenting this pertinent information will help avoid complications or discrepancies about the details of the accident. It will also provide you with a written history for your files should problems surface after your vehicle has been repaired to its pre-accident condition.

# COMMON AUTOMOTIVE MYTHS

Grandma used to say that cod liver oil cured everything that ailed a person. Well, with all due respect to her, you can't believe *everything* you hear! Take for example the many automotive myths that abound:

- *It's a good idea to let your car "warm up" in the morning.*

  It's not necessary. Start driving gently after about the first thirty seconds. In extremely cold (below zero) temperature you may let it warm up a little longer. A prolonged warm-up period in the morning wastes fuel, adds to air pollution, and will not help your engine in any way.

- *It's easier on your automatic transmission if you put it into neutral every time you stop.*

  This does not have any positive effect on your transmission, and the constant gear changing may even have an adverse effect on the life of your transmission. With manual transmissions, you'll notice less wear if you leave your car in gear (with the clutch in) while at a stop as opposed to putting it in neutral and disengaging the clutch.

- *Using cruise control increases gas consumption.*

  It has been proven that cruise control gives you the best economy because of the gradual acceleration and deceleration.

- *You'll improve fuel economy by opening the windows on hot days instead of using the air conditioner.*

  This may be true in town (if you can stand it); however, not while you're on the highway. You create wind resistance (drag) with the windows open. It takes more fuel to run at highway speeds with windows down than with the air conditioning operating.

- *Higher octane fuel helps your car start better and run better, and improves fuel economy.*

  There has been no proof to substantiate this claim for a normally running engine. Octane is simply a measure of a fuel's resistance to knocking (pinging). Use the octane rating as specified in your vehicle owner's manual.

- *Never change the brand of motor oil used in your vehicle's engine.*

  As long as you change your motor oil regularly and use an "SG"/"SH" rated oil you can use and mix any brand with another without any effect on engine life.

- *An engine sludge problem can be cured by adding a quart or two of transmission fluid to the crankcase.*

  Many felt that this did work, and it may have years ago because transmission fluid is high in detergents, and when mixed with motor oil it opened passageways inside the engine. Not so today, because of the quality of today's motor oil. You wouldn't break down sludge and you may cause emission system contamination.

- *Your car can do without the catalytic converter and the smog pump.*

  Taking off or tampering with either of these parts will not give you better gas mileage or more horsepower. Emission control systems were designed to operate with all components hooked up. Disconnecting any emissions-related device will have a negative effect on performance and fuel economy, not to mention the fact that it's illegal.

- *The air cleaner restricts air flow and robs horsepower, so remove the air cleaner element.*

  All this will do is decrease the life of your engine by as much as 50 percent. Make sure the element is clean but don't take it out. I've also seen holes drilled in air cleaner housings. This lets more hot underhood air through the air intake, which dramatically reduces power.

- *Throw away that thermostat; you don't need it.*

  That's what folks have been told to cure an overheating problem. You should never remove a thermostat and always stay with the same degree thermostat specified by the vehicle manufacturer. Without the proper temperature control (regulated by a thermostat) your car will use more fuel, run rougher, and play havoc with the emission control system.

- *If you blow a fuse, use a higher amp fuse so you're not apt to blow it again!*

  All wires and connectors were specced out with a specific amp rated fuse. If you put in a larger one, say a 30 amp for a 10 amp, you have a possibility of damaging an electronic component or causing a fire by overloading the circuit.

- *Any replacement battery will do when you need a new battery.*

  Buyer beware! You should always select a replacement battery that has the same cold cranking amp (CCA) as recommended by the vehicle manufacturer. If you opt for a budget replacement that is not up to spec, you may run into problems with your alternator, starting system, or other electrical components. You can put in a higher rated CCA battery than the original, but never go to a lower rating. You shouldn't settle for inexpensive jumper cables either. Select a quality set with a large-diameter copper cable.

- *When rotating radial ply tires, only do so front to rear, never side to side.*

  According to the major tire manufacturers it's OK to use a crisscross pattern when rotating radial ply tires (except unidirectional). Don't forget to use the spare when you rotate (if it's full sized).

- *A specific vehicle tow rating refers only to the weight of the specific item you're towing, e.g., boat, house trailer.*

  When a vehicle has the towing capacity of 5,500 lbs., that is the total load it is meant to haul. Not the weight of just a boat and trailer at 5,500 lbs. but all the things that go with it, such as fuel, water, luggage, etc. If all these things added together exceed the 5,500 lb. limit, it's likely to cause a driving situation that is completely out of balance and could lead to a serious accident. Salespeople will sometimes say you don't need to watch the load too carefully, but you do, because in the event of an accident, this overweight will be taken into consideration by an investigating officer.

- *Regularly scheduled lube jobs are essential.*

  Very few newer cars have chassis designed with lubrication points (zerk fittings). Most of the cars today require no chassis lubrication for at least 100,000 miles.

- *Sometimes a technician will say "I can't do anything about the way your car is running, it's computer controlled."*

  This has been a common response when a fast idle condition exists on a late-model car. This is a cop-out and the technician should check for problem areas like vacuum leaks. It's not always true that a computer problem is unrepairable.

- *For the cleanest engine, have it steam cleaned.*

    I don't recommend it with any vehicle because today's cars have all of the electronics stuffed under the hood. The hot steam can severely damage electronic components, and shorten the life of your hoses, wiring, and connectors. There are some excellent waterless engine cleaners on the market that will be kind to your engine components.

- *A car just runs better when it's clean.*

    Washing your car doesn't have any effect on performance. But one study pointed out that drivers of clean cars have fewer accidents. Maybe we should only drive our vehicles when they're spotless!

# SECTION ONE

□ □ □

# UNDER THE HOOD

1. WINDSHIELD WASHER RESERVOIR
2. AIR CONDITIONING COMPRESSOR
3. HEATER HOSE
4. AUTOMATIC TRANSMISSION FLUID LEVEL CHECK
5. HEATER CORE
6. AIR FILTER
7. CARBURETOR
8. DISTRIBUTOR
9. VACUUM OR POWER BRAKE UNIT
10. MASTER CYLINDER
11. STEERING COLUMN
12. SPARK PLUGS/WIRES
13. SUSPENSION STRUT
14. EXHAUST MANIFOLD
15. FUSE BOX
16. POWER STEERING
17. BATTERY
18. LOWER RADIATOR HOSE
19. POWER STEERING PUMP
20. OIL LEVEL DIP STICK
21. ALTERNATOR
22. DRIVE BELTS
23. WATER PUMP
24. THERMOSTAT HOUSING
25. FUEL LINE FILTER
26. RADIATOR
27. RADIATOR CAP
28. RADIATOR COOLANT RESERVOIR
29. UPPER RADIATOR HOSE

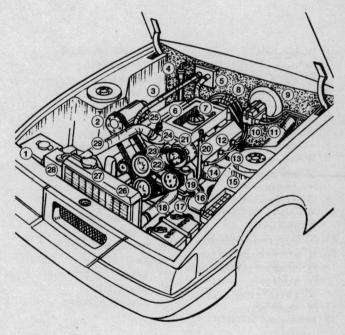

Art by Tim Kreger

1. HEADLIGHT
2. AIR CONDITIONING COMPRESSOR
3. FUEL LINE FILTER
4. AIR FILTER HOUSING
5. CARBURETOR OR FUEL INJECTION
6. ALTERNATOR
7. SPARK PLUG/PLUG WIRES
8. DISTRIBUTOR
9. MASTER CYLINDER
10. VACUUM OR POWER BRAKE UNIT
11. STEERING COLUMN
12. UNIVERSAL JOINT
13. MUFFLER/EXHAUST SYSTEM
14. DIFFERENTIAL
15. FUEL TANK
16. SHOCK ABSORBER
17. FRAME MEMBER
18. TAILLIGHT
19. TAILPIPE
20. LEAF SPRING
21. DRIVESHAFT
22. CATALYTIC CONVERTER
23. TRANSMISSION
24. DISC BRAKE CALIPER
25. DISC BRAKE ROTOR
26. STRUT
27. STABILIZER
28. POWER STEERING PUMP
29. DRIVE BELT
30. FAN
31. STEERING TIE ROD
32. RADIATOR
33. FRAME MEMBER

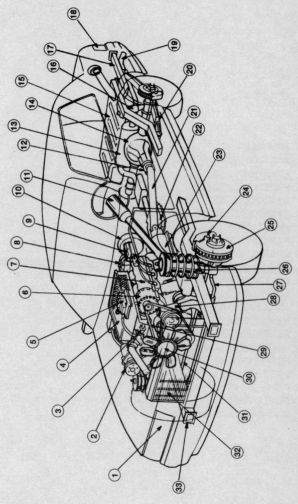

Art by Tim Kreger

# A COMPLETE TUNE-UP

❏ ❏ ❏

Your vehicle's ignition system provides the spark to ignite the air/fuel mixture in the engine's combustion chamber. A tune-up consists of ignition system parts being installed, checked, adjusted, or cleaned to bring your engine back to manufacturer's specifications, which allows the engine to run at peak efficiency.

In this chapter we'll discuss the following:
- What a tune-up is and what driveability problems indicate it's time for a tune-up
- The ignition system, different types
- Distributor assembly inspection
- Spark plugs—inspection and replacement
- Spark plug wires inspection and replacement
- Other tune-up tests and adjustments

One of the main reasons people bring their vehicles into my shop for a tune-up is that they are experiencing some kind of "driveability" problem: starting, knocking, stalling, power loss, poor gas mileage, dieseling, exhaust odor, or rough running. These symptoms indicate that a tune-up is necessary. They seldom are cured with a new set of spark plugs or a few turns of the screwdriver.

# HARD STARTING

This is the most common form of car trouble. If the starter cranks the engine, the battery is probably OK. The culprit could be a starting sensor (on fuel injected models) or the choke mechanism (on engines with carburetors). Frequently, starting failure can be traced to an electronic component or a computer controlling the ignition system.

# KNOCKING (PINGING)

This noise generally is heard when the engine is working hard, such as when accelerating or climbing a hill. While it often may be caused by a tankful of inferior gas, ignition knock (pinging) frequently is a sign your engine needs attention. It also can be caused by a buildup of carbon inside the engine.

Most late-model cars are equipped with a knock sensor which "hears" the sound and makes corrective adjustments. But this sensor cannot compensate for a severe malfunction, a condition that can affect engine performance, even damage the engine.

# STALLING

Stalling can be caused by incorrect idle speed adjustments, a malfunctioning sensor or switch, dirty fuel system parts, worn spark plugs, or other engine deficiencies.

Important things to note for a proper diagnosis of the problem:

Does it stall when . . .
- Hot?
- Cold?
- With air conditioning on?

Always remember to make note of when it happens and advise your technician.

## POWER LOSS

If your vehicle is sluggish, has a hard time accelerating, or just won't get out of its own way, you're experiencing a power loss. The engine power has been reduced, usually because of a restriction.

How long since the fuel filter was changed? A dirty filter or catalytic converter is a common cause of power loss. As noted under "Poor Gas Mileage," there can be many causes of this condition, most of which can be located with a simple diagnostic procedure.

## POOR GAS MILEAGE

By keeping a regular check of gas mileage (miles driven divided by gallons used) you can tell if your engine is losing efficiency. An efficiency drop could be caused by ignition timing out of adjustment, looseness of timing chains or belts, or a bad automatic fan clutch. Increased gas consumption may be accompanied by other symptoms, so besides the increase in fuel costs, you may have a component that if left unattended could cost you a big repair down the road or even leave you stranded.

*Note:* Poor gas mileage also may be due to
- Under-inflated tires
- Engine running too cold
- Transmission malfunction (not shifting at the precise time)
- Dragging brakes (not releasing properly after applying brakes)
- Misaligned wheels

## DIESELING

This also is known as "after-run." The engine keeps chugging and coughing for several seconds or more after the ignition is shut off. Causes can range from inferior gas to excessive idle speed.

Carbon in the combustion chamber may cause dieseling also.

## EXHAUST ODOR

A smell like rotten eggs comes from the catalytic converter, part of your car's emissions control system, when there is an engine problem or when the catalytic converter itself is malfunctioning.

## ROUGH RUNNING

A malfunction in either the fuel or ignition system can cause an engine to run roughly. It also can be due to an internal engine condition, such as a bad valve or piston.

*Note:*
• Does it occur when idling?
• When accelerating?
• At all speeds?

Your best bet is to have a qualified technician perform diagnostic and tune-up services, as needed.

Now that I've discussed the symptoms that indicate a tune-up being necessary, let's get into the heart of the matter, which is your car's ignition system, how it works and what you can do.

The old fashioned tune-up has changed considerably over

the years because of the improved equipment on modern cars and trucks. Automakers have replaced the most fragile mechanical parts of the ignition system—the points—with non-moving electronic parts. Electronic ignition, computerized engine controls, and electronic fuel injection are among the most significant automotive developments since the automobile was introduced (I'm sure you'll agree if you have ever had the "pleasure" of adjusting or installing a set of points.)

Even with all of that electronic and computerized equipment under your hood, your car still requires some loving care. A new car might be okay for a while without much attention, but it probably won't be in top running condition. Without regular maintenance, after a couple of years you may be in for some costly repairs, or even a major breakdown. A lot of a technician's attention during a tune-up will be focused on the ignition system.

The ignition system, one of the many electrical systems in your car, is primarily designed to ignite the air/fuel mixture

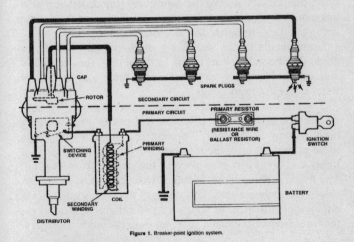

Figure 1. Breaker-point ignition system.

*Power Path Wire and Cable.*
*Used with permission.*

that is sent into the engine through the carburetor, or fuel injection system, and thereby starts your car.

The primary (or low-voltage circuit) and secondary (or high-voltage circuit) make up the ignition system. These two circuits function together and depend on each other to operate the engine.

Although there are many different ignition systems on the market today, most can be placed in one of three groups: conventional breaker-point ignitions, in use since the early 1900s; electronic ignitions, popular since the early 1970s; and distributorless ignitions, which have recently been introduced to the marketplace.

# BREAKER-POINT IGNITION SYSTEMS

With conventional breaker-point ignition, the low-voltage (primary) circuit consists of the battery, ignition switch, the primary part of the ignition coil (the coil has a dual function), the primary side of the distributor (the distributor also has a dual function), and the wires connecting each of these components to complete the electrical circuitry.

Components of the secondary (high-voltage) circuit include the secondary part of the ignition coil, the secondary side of the distributor (distributor cap, rotor, and secondary wires), and the spark plugs.

The conventional breaker-point ignition system has several disadvantages. For instance, the points must carry a high current (2–6 amp). This current gradually destroys these points, causing them to become burned and pitted; at times this condition may prevent the engine from starting. The nylon rubbing block becomes worn as it passes over the rotating distributor cam. This changes the timing and affects engine performance. In short, a more reliable ignition system or a frequent (twice a year) tune-up becomes necessary.

## ELECTRONIC IGNITION SYSTEMS

With the advent of emission controls on cars, the ignition system must operate at peak efficiency for long periods of time with little maintenance. As previously discussed, the breaker points of an ignition system become burned, pitted, and worn with time. All these problem areas reduce ignition system efficiency and cause an increase in unburned hydrocarbons, which pollute the atmosphere. For this reason, many car manufacturers have replaced the standard breaker-point system with the more reliable, maintenance-free, electronic ignition system. Owners of older cars can convert to this type of ignition system available in the aftermarket.

## DISTRIBUTORLESS IGNITION SYSTEMS

A newer type of ignition system, recently introduced to the marketplace, is the distributorless ignition, which eliminates the moving parts (e.g., points, condenser, distributor cap, distributor shaft bearings, rotor, distributor pickup) that wear out and cause problems. In theory, no distributor means:

- No timing adjustment
- No cracks from burned distributor caps
- No eroded or burned distributor rotor buttons
- No moisture accumulation inside distributor cap to cause hard starting
- No distributor components to wear out

In this system, sensors send voltage data to the underhood onboard computer. The computer sends control signals to the low-voltage sides of the ignition coils. The spark plugs are fired directly from the coils. Spark timing is controlled by an ignition module and the engine computer. About the only parts that can deteriorate on this system are the plug wires, connectors, and spark plugs.

When the ignition system is operating correctly, the voltage it produces in the secondary circuit will be high enough so that a hot spark will jump the small gap between the spark plug electrodes, igniting the compressed air/fuel mixture in the cylinder and starting the car.

# SERVICING VEHICLES WITH CONVENTIONAL BREAKER-POINT IGNITION SYSTEMS

Since there are many older vehicles on the road that use a conventional breaker-point ignition, let's look at the maintenance required for these cars. (Electronic ignition systems are virtually maintenance-free.)

The distributor sends high-energy electricity to each spark plug at the correct time for proper combustion of the fuel. The distributor cap and distributor rotor need to be inspected during a tune-up (a job you should be able to perform). This is especially important during wet, cold times of the year because of the possibility of moisture getting inside your distributor, resulting in poor performance and a possible loss of power.

## CHECKING THE DISTRIBUTOR

1. Remove the distributor cap by "popping" the spring clamps and loosening the screw clamps or screws, depending on which type cap is on your vehicle.
2. It shouldn't be necessary to remove the center coil wire or plug wires from the cap tower. You should have enough wire slack to look inside the cap.
3. Inside the cap you'll find metal spikes directly under where the plug wire connects to the outside of the cap.

You'll also find a soft carbon (non-metal) post under the coil wire connection. This post has a convex end that protrudes out of the distributor cap and contacts the center of the rotor when the cap is reinstalled.

4. Take a close look inside the cap. Check that the metal spikes are not burned and do not show corrosion. Also check the carbon post end that contacts the rotor, for de-

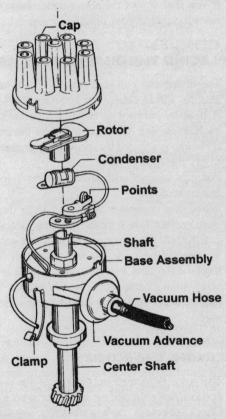

Cap

Rotor

Condenser

Points

Shaft

Base Assembly

Vacuum Hose

Vacuum Advance

Clamp

Center Shaft

*Art by Tim Kreger*

terioration (flat or broken), and check for cracks in the distributor cap.

5. Inspect the outside of the cap for cracks or damage. Pay close attention to the spark plug wire connectors.

6. Finally, check the inside and outside of the cap for any black lines running from the outside plug wire connection point, or the inside metal spike. These are known as carbon tracks.

7. If you find any of the above conditions outlined, you'll need to replace your distributor cap.

## REPLACING THE DISTRIBUTOR CAP

1. The distributor cap is secured to the housing by screw clamps, spring clamps, or ordinary screws.

2. If held by screw clamps, use a screwdriver and turn each screw one half turn to release the cap.

3. If the cap is secured by spring clamps, use a screwdriver to pry the springs loose.

4. For caps secured with ordinary screws, loosen until cap can be removed.

5. When you remove a plug wire from the old cap, you must replace that wire in the same location on the new cap. Repeat the process until all wires are in place. And be sure to push each wire down securely in the new cap.

6. Replace the new cap and tighten with screwdriver for screw clamps and screw-type housings. You should be able to snap on spring clamps with simple hand pressure.

## CHECKING THE ROTOR

1. The rotor is located on the top of the distributor shaft and is simply slipped on and off or is secured by screws.

2. Check for cracks, carbon tracks, or any signs of burning on the metallic part of the top of the rotor.

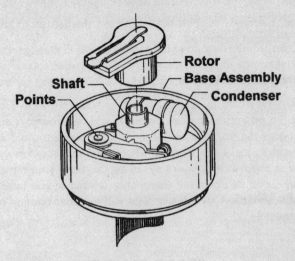

*Art by Tim Kreger*

3. If any of the above conditions are seen on your rotor, re-place it.
4. Just make sure the new rotor slips onto the distributor shaft in the exact way the old rotor came off. The metal finger has to be pointing to the same location inside the distributor cap or the car will not run.

As a final check for your distributor, take hold of the distributor shaft (with cap off) and try to move it side to side. It should not move. If it's loose, you may need a new or re-built distributor.

## REPLACING BREAKER POINTS

While all components are important in a conventional ig-nition system, the breaker points are the most likely to cause an engine to run poorly. The inspection, readjustment, or re-placement of these points is a very precise, delicate procedure. I strongly suggest that you leave this job up to your professional technician.

## IGNITION SWITCH

On older cars, an ignition switch had only one job—turning the primary electrical circuit on and off. Today, it also activates the starter motor, connects the alternator and accessories, locks the steering wheel, and lets you know if you're about to lock your keys in the car. Have your technician check its operation thoroughly whenever you have a major service. A switch that fails will cut your ignition off completely.

## SPARK PLUGS

A spark plug is nothing more than two wires close enough together so that a spark can jump between them (known as the "business end" of your ignition system). The electricity that will jump the gap between the wires comes from the distributor. It flows through the ceramic-encased wire and jumps to the other wire, which is connected to a ground to complete the circuit.

When your plugs are worn out, your car will start misfiring or running rough. You'll have difficulty in the morning starting it up, you may not have the power you once had to merge into freeway traffic, and your mileage will suffer. Therefore, your spark plugs and plug wires should be inspected every 6,000 miles.

You can learn plenty about your vehicle's engine condition by carefully inspecting your spark plugs. You can find evidence of excessive fuel and oil consumption, a fuel shortage in the combustion chamber, cylinder-to-cylinder balance, and an indication of a potential problem.

## REMOVING SPARK PLUGS

1. Your engine should be cool, if not cold, when attempting to remove plugs (a hot engine could take as many as two hours to cool down). This will prevent any accidental contact with hot engine parts, like the exhaust manifold. This is also especially important on engines that have aluminum alloy cylinder heads.

2. An additional safeguard is to disconnect the battery (negative side off first).

3. Remove the spark plug wires from the plugs only by holding the boot (the part that fits over the plug), twisting to loosen, and pulling off. Never pull on the wires themselves—you'll damage the insides, which will significantly shorten the life of the wires!

4. Remember where each wire is to be reinstalled. It's sometimes confusing since some wires are nearly equal in length. I've used common clothespins that I've numbered and attached to the wires to help in remembering proper locations.

5. Purchase a special spark plug socket to remove each plug. These have a rubber insert that will prevent damage to the ceramic insulator and provide easier removal and replacement of the plug.

6. Place the socket over the plug and press down to secure a snug fit. First loosen the plug one or two turns only, for road dust and grip removal.

7. Whether you're a trained technician or not, an absolute must is to clean the cavity of the spark plug area before removing the plug.

   There is no magic cleaning solution, but this cleaning method won't cost you a dime: *Use air pressure.* You may use a bicycle pump or blow into a tube to eliminate all dust and dirt as well as loose stones, screws, bolts, nuts, and washers. If all of this foreign material is not cleaned out of the spark plug cavity and falls instead into the engine cylinder, the piston and/or cylinder head may be damaged and you'll have *big* problems.

8. Carefully loosen and remove each plug, and place on your workbench in order of removal, so you'll know which cylinder the plug came out of during inspection.

## SPARK PLUG INSPECTION

Maybe you can't tell a book by its cover, but you can tell a lot about your engine by what's covering the tips of your spark plugs. Indeed, experienced mechanics often "read" the working ends of spark plugs to evaluate engine performance.

One factor that makes spark plugs especially telling about an engine's internal functioning is that a plug is attached to each cylinder. For that reason, it's important to note what cylinder each spark plug has come from. Spark plugs can often indicate where an engine's having trouble, what the problem is, and how to take care of it.

There's nothing mysterious about what spark plugs have to say; their language is straightforward. With that in mind, here is a primer, of sorts, to help you learn that language, courtesy of AlliedSignal Automotive Aftermarket/Autolite:

Normal plug

**Normal Plug:** It's completely normal for a spark plug insulator tip, center electrode, and ground electrode (the last of which looks like a curled-over finger) to take on a slight gray tint. If a plug comes out with such a tint, and is dry to the touch, everything should be normal in its cylinder.

Red Coating

**Red Coating:** Sometimes the ground electrode, the center tip, and the ceramic insulator around the tip take on a pinkish-red hue. The red

coating comes from additives used in some unleaded gasolines, and doesn't indicate a problem.

**Worn Plug:** The outlines of the
ground electrode, center tip, and ceramic insulator should be clean and
sharply defined. Signs of heavy ero-
sion of any of their surfaces indicate
worn-out spark plugs that should be
replaced.

Worn Plug

**Glazing:** When a spark plug's ceramic insulator appears to have a
melted coating, the plug is glazed.
Glazing occurs when fouling deposits melt because the plug becomes too hot at high speeds.
Switching to a colder-heat-range
spark plug should solve the problem.

Glazing

**Carbon Fouling:** Carbon fouling
is the opposite problem. It can be
caused by using spark plugs that are
too cold, by extensive low-speed
driving, rich fuel mixture, weak ignition, or oil consumption. Carbon fouling shows up as a black, sooty coating

Carbon Fouling

on the spark plug. Failure to correct the cause of carbon fouling will shorten the life of your spark plugs, and the engine
will be hard to start.

Recommendations for your technician should be.
• Check for correct plug heat range first.
• *On carbureted engines,* check for choke and choke
  pull-off malfunctioning and/or improper adjustment.
  *On fuel-injected engines,* check for clogged injectors,
  and the cold-start valve. Also check for correct fuel-
  pressure specs. *On computer-controlled engines,*
  check all input signals to the computer, including temperature sensors.

- *On all engines,* check for severe vacuum leaks, weak spark or low voltage output and carbon canister/purge valve operation.
- Problem could also result from continuous low-speed driving or poor cylinder compression.

Lead Fouling

**Lead Fouling:** (Not as common today because of the leaded fuel phase-out). A lead-fouled spark plug appears to have had a rough coat of plaster applied to parts of the center electrode and insulator. Lead fouling occurs on plugs used in engines that burn leaded fuel; when big enough deposits build up, the plug will short out. Lead fouling is not an indicator of other problems, and has become rare lately due to the cutback on the amount of lead used in gasoline. I recommend plug replacement.

Fuel Fouling

**Fuel Fouling:** The working areas of a fuel-fouled spark plug tend to be damp with gasoline; you can usually smell the fuel right on the plug, and the insulator is often tinted the color of charcoal. A fuel-fouled plug indicates that the cylinder it came from can't use all the gasoline it's getting. If all the spark plugs show signs of fuel fouling, look for a sticking carburetor choke. A sticking choke may be cured by using carburetor cleaner on the choke linkage, or it could be an electrical problem, for which your technician will need to assist. If only one plug or a few are fuel fouled, chances are the problem is in the ignition system, though one or more fuel injectors could be leaking.

Occasionally, fuel fouling is caused by using spark plugs of too cold a heat range. Cars driven primarily in stop-and-go traffic are especially likely to need hotter spark plugs in order to control fuel fouling. The causes of fuel fouling, if allowed to go on unchecked, can lead to the diluting of your motor oil with gasoline, which leads to rapid wear inside the engine.

**Oil Fouling:** If a spark plug appears to have been dipped in black, greasy mud, which was then baked into a crust, it's oil fouled. The engine needs repairs: Piston rings, valve guides, and/or valve seals are badly worn and in need of replacement.

Oil Fouling

**Detonation:** If a spark plug has worn surfaces on either its tip or its electrode, and/or if pieces of the insulator have been blown or chipped away, the plug is shouting *"Do something right away."* It has been physically damaged by detonation. If the cause of that detonation isn't fixed, the same forces that damaged the spark plug will damage engine parts that can't be replaced as readily. Usually, retarding the ignition timing or switching to a higher-octane fuel will take care of the problem.

Detonation

Pre-Ignition

Courtesy of AlliedSignal Automotive Aftermarket/Autolite.

**Pre-Ignition:** Pre-ignition can lead to the same types of internal engine damage as detonation, but it happens much faster. It generally shows up in the form of burned or melted electrodes. Often, just changing to a colder plug will take care of the problem. Sometimes, ignition timing must be retarded, or the fuel/air mixture must be enriched.

Although most of the spark plug conditions reviewed above indicate a problem, bad spark plugs usually won't mean an expensive repair.

Only one of these examples, the oil-fouled plug, indicates need for extensive work. In the case of other abnormal spark plugs, only minor adjustments are needed. But those corrections shouldn't be put off. At the least, leaving the engine out of adjustment wastes gasoline and efficiency. At worst, leaving things alone can ruin a good engine that could have been saved by minor work.

## REINSTALLING SPARK PLUGS

Considering the time you've spent in removing and inspecting your old plugs, you may choose to install a new set of plugs. If your old set is in good shape and with only five to six thousand miles since installed (about six months), you may opt to clean the electrodes with a wire

### HERE'S A SIMPLE WAY TO TIGHTEN SPARK PLUGS PROPERLY

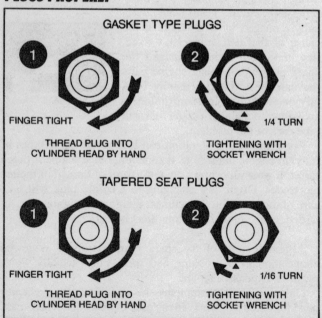

GASKET TYPE PLUGS

1 — FINGER TIGHT
THREAD PLUG INTO CYLINDER HEAD BY HAND

2 — 1/4 TURN
TIGHTENING WITH SOCKET WRENCH

TAPERED SEAT PLUGS

1 — FINGER TIGHT
THREAD PLUG INTO CYLINDER HEAD BY HAND

2 — 1/16 TURN
TIGHTENING WITH SOCKET WRENCH

*Champion Spark Plugs. Used with permission.*

brush, regap with a special tool, and let them go for another 6,000 miles.

1. Use anti-seizing compound (lubricant) on plug threads prior to installation. This will allow easy removal from the head, especially aluminum heads.
2. After being gapped to manufacturer's specifications (the gap is measured in thousands of an inch with a special tool from your auto parts store), place each new plug into the cylinder *by hand.*
3. Finger-tighten the plug, after you've jiggled it while screwing it in to make sure the threads are properly matched. For hard-to-reach cylinders, slip a rubber hose (that can bend 90 degrees) over the spark plug to help start threading the plug. The hose has to grab the plug snugly.
4. For gasket-type plugs, tighten plug with the plug socket one-quarter turn after it has been finger-tightened.
5. For tapered-seat plugs, tighten plug with socket only one-sixteenth of a turn after finger-tight.
6. Attach each plug wire by pushing the rubber firmly over the tip of the plug by hand until you feel the positive connection.

## SPARK PLUG WIRES

Spark plug wires like any other part, wear out with age, abuse, or through the effects of the environment. While other electrical components are routinely checked, spark plug wires are often overlooked. Yet, one bad plug wire can cause rough idling and poor acceleration and cut your gas mileage. Here are a few easy ways to locate faulty spark plug wires that don't show obvious physical damage.

**Heat Damage:** Engine heat can burn insulation and boots. A damaged boot can prevent proper sealing and affect performance. Damaged insulation allows voltage to jump to

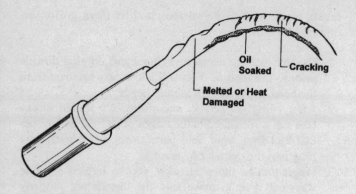

Oil Soaked

Cracking

Melted or Heat Damaged

Art by Tim Kruger

ground. If wire is stiff and brittle from age, it should also be replaced.

**Abrasion Damage:** Wire rubbing against engine parts, particularly sharp edges, can cause cuts and breaks in insulation that will allow voltage to jump to ground instead of reaching the spark plug.

**Vibration Damage:** Constant wear and tear caused by engine vibration can loosen the electrical connection and reduce the spark before it reaches the plug. Loose connections also create heat buildup which damages the conductor.

## SPARK PLUG WIRE REPLACEMENT

1. Turn off the ignition and let the engine cool (usually two hours is enough).
2. Remove and replace one wire at a time, starting with the longest wire. When removing wires from the plug or distributor cap, twist the boot to loosen it from the plug. Do not jerk or tug on the wires or you may break the connection. Pull on the boot or use a tool designed for this purpose.

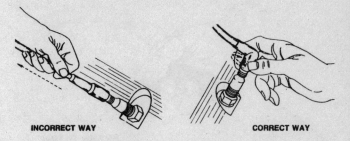

INCORRECT WAY                                      CORRECT WAY

*Power Path Wire and Cable. Used with permission.*

3. Match the longest wire in the new set with the longest old wire, then match the next longest, etc. Do not match the identical length, as this varies with different wire manufacturers.
4. Make sure the wire end seats all the way down into the distributor cap. Pinch the edge of the nipple gently to let out the excess air; otherwise the nipple may not seal properly or may push the wire out of the cap.

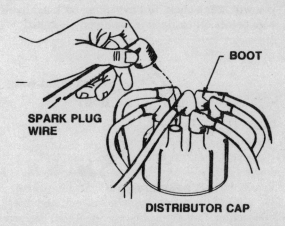

BOOT

SPARK PLUG
WIRE

DISTRIBUTOR CAP

*Power Path Wire and Cable. Used with permission.*

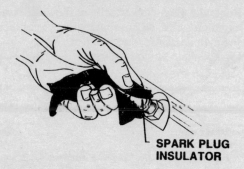

**SPARK PLUG
INSULATOR**

*Power Path Wire and Cable. Used with permission.*

5. Wipe off the spark plug insulator and distributor cap
   towers before installing new wires.
6. When installing the spark plug end, push the wire on the
   plug, hold the end of the boot and continue gently pushing and twisting. The end should snap on firmly, with
   the boot over the plug insulator. Do not force the wire.
   When correctly aligned, the wire will go on easily and
   you will hear a click. Test by pulling back lightly; if the
   wire comes off easily, it is improperly installed.

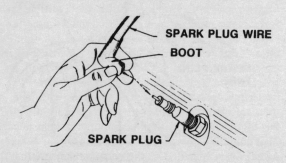

**SPARK PLUG WIRE**

**BOOT**

**SPARK PLUG**

*Power Path Wire and Cable. Used with permission.*

7. Route the plug wires exactly as they were originally. To avoid crossfire, do not route wires of consecutively firing cylinders next to each other.
8. Change the coil wire whenever replacing an entire set.

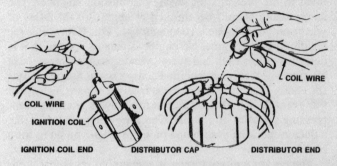

*Power Path Wire and Cable. Used with permission.*

9. If necessary, replace the spark plug wire separator to hold the spark plug wires in position in relation to one another and keep them away from the hot exhaust manifolds or other metal objects. This protects them from the heat of the manifolds and reduces capacitive coupling between the conductor and metal surfaces. Capacitive coupling can load down the ignition system and cause a misfire on engines that need a tune-up.
10. Never clamp secondary spark plug wires tightly or allow them to be pinched between the air cleaner and the distributor. The high-voltage stresses will be increased at these points and hasten wire failure.
11. Never bundle spark plug wires together with tape, pull them through metal tubes, or dress them tightly against the engine. This may look neat, but could cause capacitive coupling, crossfiring, or misfiring.
12. After you've installed all the wires, make sure that they are clear of choke or throttle linkages, hot exhaust manifolds, and sharp metal edges.

# OTHER TUNE-UP TESTS AND ADJUSTMENTS

An engine's compression ratio is the amount of pressure applied to the fuel mixture in the combustion chamber. The compression should be checked at about 30,000 miles or whenever your engine is running rough. This test reveals the condition of an engine. No engine is able to operate as it is designed unless each and every cylinder is operating at peak efficiency—that is, at specified compression. Specifications for compression are found in pounds per square inch (psi). For example, a particular engine may have a cranking compressing pressure of 150 psi. Checking compression is like a doctor checking your blood pressure when you go in for a physical exam.

The reason ignition timing is essential to set is that it ensures that each spark plug fires at the exact moment for maximum engine efficiency.

The above two procedures are involved, especially for today's automobile, and are best left to your technician.

# MOTORING TIP

## HISSES, CLUNKS, AND HESITATIONS

Few things in life are as frustrating as retrieving your car from a visit to the shop, driving it home, and discovering along the way that problems you asked them to repair have not been corrected. And believe me, from a technician's point of view, it's frustrating for most of us, too. How can we improve our lines of communication with each other?

My tip is to place a motoring journal and a writing instrument in a handy spot in the car and use it to make notes of peculiar noises or vibrations, electrical problems, service lights blinking, etc. Anything and everything you and your technician may need to make an accurate diagnosis.

This will save time, energy, and Excedrin tablets for everyone involved.

In shops around the country one of the most common repairs attempted is to eliminate that pesky noise under the hood that drives motorists crazy. And I know from my forty years of adding up repair orders, folks sure do pay technicians like me a lot to perform the detective work necessary to locate the problem. I have a suggestion that will save you some money and time.

You should try to locate the problem *prior* to seeing your repair shop. This can be done with a couple of common household items. For finding metal-to-metal knocks, clunks, or clanks, use a long screwdriver (twenty-four inches or so). With the handle up to your ear touch the blade of the screwdriver to the various components under the hood while the engine is running. The noise will travel up the blade and to your ear.

For hissing sounds, such as exhaust and vacuum leaks, use a three-quarter-inch-diameter heater hose or a section of an old garden hose cut to a three to four foot section. Repeat the same procedure as outlined above.

When doing your own diagnosis, be extra careful around the engine while it is running. Have someone inside the vehicle with a foot on the brake, and block all wheels.

Who knows, you may even be able to repair the problem yourself and save yourself a visit to your repair shop. Now for you mobile office owners.

What an exciting time for all of you who make your living out of your car. There are so many aftermarket accessories you can add to your "company on wheels." Do you remember when the only accessory you could run was an electric shaver plugged into your cigarette lighter? Now you can add everything from alarm systems to fax machines, along with your telephone, of course.

However, you may have noticed a difference in the way your vehicle is running now that you've plugged into your car's electrical system.

I've seen instances where, especially with late-model "computerized" cars, the "black box" has picked up the RF (radio frequency) signals from aftermarket accessories and affected the idle and acceleration of certain vehicles. These mystery RF signals can result in an engine power surge. Double-check with your accessory installer if your car suffers from these symptoms.

# BELTS, CHAINS, AND HOSES

□ □ □

In this chapter we'll discuss those items under the hood that drive important components and carry the fluids necessary for temperature control and lubrication.

The following areas will be discussed:
- Types of automotive belts
- Belt inspection, signs of wear
- Belt care, replacement
- Types of automotive hoses
- Hose inspection, care, replacement.

When was the last time you took a look at your drive belts?

These V- and flat-shaped belts are some of the most overlooked parts on your car, and if a belt breaks, you're probably in for a costly repair or breakdown.

## TYPES OF BELTS

Three kinds of belts are found in cars: V-ribbed belts, V-belts, and timing belts. All are essential to a car's operation. Without them, a car cannot run for very long. Typically, V-ribbed belts and V-belts drive the following:

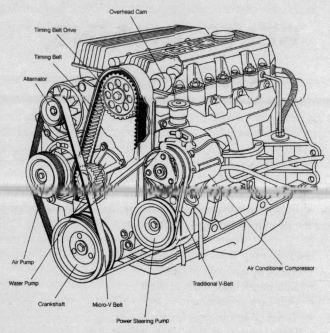

*Gates Belts and Hoses. Used with permission.*

- The alternator, which supplies electrical power to the car
- The water pump, which circulates coolant
- The fan, which draws in air that cools the coolant in the radiator
- A number of accessories, from power steering pumps, to air conditioning compressors, to air pumps that operate other auxiliary equipment

Timing belts drive the camshaft and are found primarily in smaller overhead-cam engines. (The camshaft has a series of lobes for timing the opening and closing of intake and exhaust valves.) Their use is expanding into high-performance V-6 engines, and they may also drive other components, such as injection pumps and internal water pumps.

# V-BELT DATES BACK TO 1917

In early automobiles, fans and alternators were turned by a round hemp rope or a flat belt made of leather or rubber. In 1917, John G. Gates invented the V-belt—a wedge-shaped rubber belt that fit more efficiently into the V-shaped trough of pulleys. As cars evolved, so did their belts.

Rubber compounds were developed to resist winter's brittle cold and summer's scorching heat. These compounds also had to resist engine heat, engine oil, coolant, and road debris, such as dirt and water. In addition, belts had to perform almost contrasting functions: They had to be flexible enough to transmit power smoothly around pulleys that traveled more than a thousand revolutions per minute, and they had to be structurally strong enough to handle the needed tension on the belt drive.

## V-BELT INSPECTION

Belts are built to be resilient and flexible, but they are not as durable as metal. After a few years, heat, oil, high mileage, and stress take their toll.

Old drive belts may become loose and slip. A slipping belt doesn't turn pulleys efficiently, and the friction generated causes the belt to overheat. The overheated belt can transfer its heat to the pulley and overheat the bearing lubricants, leading to accessory damage. The worst potential damage, however, is that loose or lost belts can cause engines to overheat.

Wear on a bandless belt is often difficult to detect. (Until about the mid-1970s, most V-belts featured a protective fabric cover or band on the outside.)

Ideally, all drive belts should be inspected once a month for wear and proper tension. Tests have shown that the chance of V-belt failure goes up dramatically the fourth year of service. That's why I remind consumers to replace their belts, regardless of how they look, every three years or 30,000 miles.

Many belts fail before four years if they are experiencing excessive wear and tear. How fast a belt wears is also determined by its function. Alternator and air conditioning drives are demanding on belts. Power steering and water pumps are less so. Often the first indication of a faulty belt or faulty tensioning is a squeaking noise coming from under the hood. While this may be a warning, it is not a reliable indicator of damage.

## SIGNS OF WEAR FOR V-BELTS

**Glazed or Shiny Sidewalls:** The friction created by a loose belt slipping in the pulley causes the belt sidewalls to become slick and shiny. These glazed sidewalls lose their gripping strength and the belt slips even more. Grease and oil on the pulley can also cause this condition.

**Cracks:** Deep bottom cracks that appear at regular intervals are caused by the belt turning around a too-small pulley (usually the alternator)—the undercord is being stressed to the breaking point.

**Chunk-Out:** As cracks deepen, chunks of the belt start to break off, destroying it.

**Separating Layers:** A belt that is falling apart in layers could be a victim of oil from leaking engine parts. Oil and grease are a rubber compound's worst enemies, weakening the compound's bonds and making the belt soft and spongy. Eventually, such a belt will slip, create heat, and fail.

**Tensile Break:** A large foreign object in the pulley can cut into the belt and break the tensile cords. A tensile break may occur, but go unnoticed, when a belt is ofrced or pried on during installation.

## Glazing

Slick sidewalls lose gripping power and the belt slips.

## Cracks

Deep cracks indicate the undercord is stressed to the breaking point.

## Missing Chunks
## and Separating Layers

This damage causes the belt to slip and eventually break.

## Streaked Sidewalls

Foreign objects or a rough pulley pit the sidewalls and the belt starts slipping.

## Tensile Break

Broken cords can lead to the belt breaking.

**Pulley-Damaged Sidewall:** A rough wall on the pulley, or a foreign object (such as sand or gravel) will gouge the belt sidewall. Foreign objects can get into a pulley from an oily, sticky belt. Regular cleaning of drive components helps prevent this problem.

**Edge-Cord Failure:** When a crack develops where the tensile cord is exposed, the cord gets damaged. Too small pulleys, overtightening, and heavy accessory loads also contribute to edge-cord failure.

# NEWER CARS WITH V-RIBBED BELTS

V-ribbed belts work better in today's smaller engine compartments than conventional V-belts. This belt's construction gives it greater flexibility around smaller pulleys, and it bends more easily around the back side of pulleys. This last feature allows the ribbed V-belt to power "serpentine" drives—drives that require power to be transmitted from both sides of the belt.

One serpentine belt can replace several V-belts, taking up much less space. This enables designers to downsize engine compartments.

## V-RIBBED BELT INSPECTION

Heat, stress, and time take their toll on V-ribbed belts just as much as they do on V-belts. Slipping belts cause heat buildup, leading to potential accessory damage and/or an overheated engine.

When a V-ribbed belt on a serpentine drive breaks, it's the equivalent of as many as three regular V-belts breaking at the same time. Without the belt, the accessory drives won't work.

To help motorists avoid this unpleasant and hazardous situation, I recommend replacing a V-ribbed belt every three years or 30,000 miles, as with V-belts. (See installation tips later in this chapter.)

To inspect a belt, first make sure the engine is off. Examine the sidewalls and bottom of the belt carefully. The following are the three most common failure modes. They indicate that the belt could be near failure and therefore, should be replaced immediately:

**Cracking:** In addition to continuous exposure to high temperature, the stress of bending around the pulleys leads to cracking. As a rule, if cracks appear the belt should be replaced.

**Chunking:** When a chunk, or section of rib, breaks off a V-ribbed belt, the belt can fail at any moment.

**Pilling:** Pilling happens when material is sheared off the undercord and builds up in the belt grooves. There are numerous causes, such as lack of tension, misalignment, and/or worn pulleys. When pilling leads to belt noise or excess belt vibration, the belt should be replaced.

## Signs of Wear for V-ribbed Belts

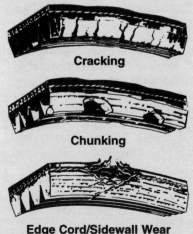

**Cracking**

**Chunking**

**Edge Cord/Sidewall Wear**

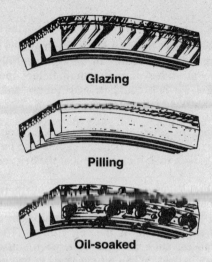

**Glazing**

**Pilling**

**Oil-soaked**

*Gates Belts and Hoses. Used with permission.*

### Cracking
Cracks along the width of the ribs are a sure sign that the belt is in its latter stages of service life. If the cracks extend down to the tensile cord, or if the belt is four years old, replace it.

### Chunking
Deep cracks will lead to chunking, where parts of the ribs will break off. Replace the belt immediately.

### Edge Cord/Sidewall Wear
This type of wear is often caused when a foreign object, such as a pebble, cuts perpendicularly into the belt, and breaks a tensile cord. Damage to the tensile cord also can occur when a belt is forced or pried on during installation. A misaligned drive will cause premature wear to the sidewall of the belt.

### Glazing
Friction, created by a loose belt slipping in the pulley, causes the belt sidewalls to become slick and shiny. The result is rapid heat aging, which accelerates cracking and eventual chunking.

**Pilling**

Pilling occurs when rubber compound from the belt wears off and settles in the apex of the V-groove. This can cause uneven rideout, vibration, and belt noise if the accumulation is severe.

**Oil-soaked**

Grease, oil, and other engine fluids on the belt sidewalls, or in the pulley grooves, will glaze the belt and increase slippage. In some cases, petroleum contamination may deteriorate rubber and lead to premature failure.

# OTHER FAILURE MODES
# FOR V-RIBBED BELTS

Three other modes are less threatening, but will reduce the service life of a belt.

**Edge Cord/Sidewall Wear:** This is often caused when a foreign object, such as a pebble, cuts perpendicularly into the belt and breaks a tensile cord. Damage to the cord also can occur when a belt is forced on or overtightened or during installation. A misaligned drive will cause premature wear to the sidewall of the belt.

**Glazing:** Friction, created by a loose belt slipping on the pulley, causes the belt sidewalls to become slick and shiny. The result is rapid heat aging, which accelerates cracking and eventual chunking.

Glazing on the top cover of the belt normally results from improper tension. The locked center (manual) tensioner (keeps belt tight) may have to be readjusted, or the automatic tensioning may need replacing.

**Oil Contamination:** Grease, oil, and other engine fluids on the belt sidewalls or in the pulley grooves will glaze the belt and increase slippage. In most cases, petroleum contamination will deteriorate rubber and lead to premature failure.

# NOISY BELTS?

One indicator of belt wear, and impending failure, is belt noise—those annoying squeaks, squeals, chirps, and growls coming from under the hood.

Older belts become smoother, creating a glossy, glazed surface, which raises the likelihood of noise. Different noises can mean different kinds of problems, however.

**Chirping:** Belt "chirping" (an intermittent, high-pitched, birdlike noise that can be heard as the engine is revved up) usually indicates pulley misalignment.

**Squealing:** "Squealing" is a more continuous sound that commonly occurs when pulling away from a stop, and usually suggests incorrect belt tension.

Belt squeal also occurs momentarily when the car is started after it has sat idle for a time, such as overnight.

As the belt turns on the drive, it heats up. Then, it shrinks enough that the tension reaches its normal level, and the squeal stops.

Squealing can also occur when higher strain is placed on the engine. For example, the belt runs fine until the air conditioner is turned on.

**Slapping:** A "slapping" sound is likely to be caused by either loose belts, which need to be retensioned, or misalignment of a belt.

# IDENTIFYING BELT CONTAMINATION
## (V-Ribbed Belts)

Contamination of the belt drive is perhaps the easiest cause of belt noise to identify, but may take the help of a service technician.

The belt should be inspected for oil contamination or road grit in the belt grooves. Gravel will sometimes be pushed through to the back side of the belt, and the holes may be

visible on the cover. Dirt accumulation on the belt may also
be obvious.

A properly tightened belt on a well-aligned drive should
provide quiet and trouble-free service for many miles. If the
noise persists, or if the belt is over three years old, change it
immediately.

## INSTALLATION TIPS FOR REPLACING V-BELTS AND V-RIBBED BELTS

- Disconnect the car battery to prevent a problem with
  the fan blades. (You could lose the presets from the
  memory on accessories like radio and car phone.)
- Check the alignment of the pulleys (using a straight
  edge), since they may be contributing to the problem.
- Don't use a tool to pry off the old belt. Instead, loosen
  the mounting-bracket pivoting-adjustment bolt. Push
  the pulley toward the engine block. You should now
  be able to remove the old belt by hand, without damage to any of the pulleys.
- Make sure you have the correct size belt for the job
  you are doing.
- Invest in a tension gauge. Belts that are too loose or too
  tight are prone to quick failure. Adjusting belt tension
  "by the feel" of it just isn't good enough for today's
  belts.
- After installing the new belt, allow the car to run for
  fifteen minutes or so. Then recheck and adjust for
  proper belt tension.

## TIMING BELTS AND TIMING CHAINS

Automotive timing belts, first introduced in the mid-1960s,
have gained a broad acceptance and have gradually replaced
the formerly used timing chain. Today, more than five hun-

dred models of cars and light trucks come equipped with timing belts.

The timing belt is a combination timing chain and flat belt that can use both its inner and outer surfaces to drive separate engine components and/or accessories.

Its inner surface is used to drive the overhead camshaft that is common to subcompact car engines. To do this, molded notches on the belt's underside mesh with the teeth on the sprockets found on the crankshaft (the main rotating shaft of the engine) and camshaft. This arrangement provides constant, slip-proof power transfer.

## WHEN A TIMING BELT BREAKS

Although timing belts are designed and engineered to withstand the high temperatures and increased rpm's of today's engines, they do eventually wear out. It's important to replace the belt before it fails, especially in cars with interference engines.

Automobile overhead-cam engines fall into two categories: free running and interference.

**INTERFERENCE**
Valve/Piston
Collision

**FREE RUNNING**
No Valve/Piston
Interference

*Goodyear Belts and Hoses. Used with permission.*

In the free-running (non-interference) engines found on many cars, there is enough clearance between the valves and pistons to prevent engine damage if the timing belt breaks, even when the cam stops with a valve fully open.

But in interference engines, a broken timing belt can cause the pistons to slam into the valves, resulting in serious damage and possibly ruining the engine, or at least causing expensive repairs.

Most cars with U.S. nameplates are free-running. Several notable exceptions are some models of the Chevy Spectrum and Chevette, the Plymouth Colt, and the Pontiac LeMans and Sunbird. The majority of these exceptions have foreign-made engines.

Most imports, however, have higher compression engines, and are most often the interference type. In all, it is estimated that nearly 40 percent of the engines requiring timing belts are interference engines. More than a dozen manufacturers, from Acura to Yugo, produce this type of engine.

## CARE AND SERVICE OF TIMING BELTS

While timing belts are manufactured with the same high-strength material as automotive V-belts, the timing belt's special design and use make it very susceptible to wear. Timing belts cannot withstand as rough a treatment as the standard V-belt and, therefore, should be checked frequently for any signs of wear damage, and retensioned when necessary by your service technician.

## TIMING BELT REPLACEMENT

It's important to replace a timing belt at its suggested replacement interval. The replacement interval most recommended by automobile manufacturers is 50,000 to 60,000 miles, or about four to five years of driving.

For optimum service, and to avoid shortened belt life, or

even premature engine failure, the replacement timing belt must be an OE-equivalent (original equipment). This means that the belt must be constructed of car-factory proven materials that resist the effects of sustained high temperatures, while providing extended durability.

## REPLACING THE TIMING CHAIN

Those of you who are keeping your favorite V-8s on the road, pushing 100,000 miles or more, must keep an eye on your car's timing chain/timing gear assembly. On today's engines, the timing chain drives the cam by connecting it to the crankshaft, allowing the valves to open and close at precise moments for efficient ignition. While it is fairly easy for your technician to check the condition of these parts, it can be very expensive for you if you wait too long and experience failure. Be sure the timing chain and gear are replaced in the 125,000- to 150,000-mile range.

# AUTOMOTIVE HOSES

When we start to consider all of the applications of hose products to various automotive systems, the list becomes impressive. They're responsible for carrying fluids, fuel, and air between components throughout the vehicle. Aside from the most obvious radiator and heater hose, the modern automobile also uses hoses in power steering and air conditioning applications, as well as in braking, fuel, and transmission systems. Hose tubing is even used in the operation of windshield washers.

Each of these applications demands special requirements. A hose that is suitable for one application will likely not be right for another. Each hose type must be able to survive the chemicals, pressure, and temperatures that are unique to that application, especially fuel injected vehicles where high-pressure fuel hoses are required. (Using an incorrect hose here will eventually cause it to burst.)

For that reason, the industry has set standards that test the ability of a hose to perform dependably in actual working conditions. Standards have been set for dimension (size), strength (burst resistance), durability, and resistance to chemicals and temperature variation. Stay with your brand-name hoses and you will be fine.

## RADIATOR HOSES

The hoses on your car's cooling system perform some very difficult and vital tasks. They transport extremely hot, pressurized coolant solution to and from the radiator during the cooling process. They also function as a shock absorber between the engine and hose connections, protecting the connections from damage and a resulting leak (and repair bill). Few other components can disable your car faster than failure of these hoses during operation.

Exposure to extreme under-the-hood temperatures, oil and grease, and the atmosphere all contribute to conditions similar to the hose pictured on next page. *Check your hose regularly* for these conditions:

- *Cracking,* usually caused by heat, aging, and weathering
- *Bulging/swelling,* usually caused by excessive heat or exposure to oil or grease
- *Spongy,* usually means the hose has been exposed to oil or grease

All of these conditions call for immediate hose replacement.

As with your engine's belts, hoses should be changed every three years or 30,000 miles.

See cooling system chapter (p. 69) for instructions on changing a radiator hose.

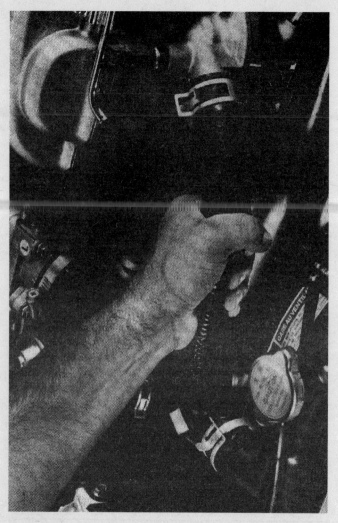

**An occasional check of cooling system parts can prevent trouble on the road.**

*Car Care Council. Used with permission.*

# THE BATTERY

□ □ □

## WORKING SAFELY ON YOUR BATTERY

Be careful when working around a car battery. All batteries emit hydrogen gas, which can be toxic. It's a good idea to wear safety goggles and rubber gloves when working on your battery. And it goes without saying, that you shouldn't smoke around the battery. **The final warning is to not wear jewelry when working on the battery. You may have instant "barbecued" fingers if your ring makes contact with the battery post.**

Inside this chapter:
- Safety tips
- Battery cleaning
- Battery cable service
- Jump starting
- Battery selection

The battery does not store electricity, as a lot of people may think. It does hold chemicals and metals that interact to produce the electricity upon demand. The colder the temperature outside or the lower the charge of the battery, the less capability the battery will have to do its job. For instance, a fully charged battery at 80°F will deliver only about 40 percent of its power at 0°F. Unfortunately, when your battery is in its weakest condition (in cold weather), it is required to do the heaviest work, turning over an engine that's been out in the cold. What can you do to keep your battery in shape and keep you on the road?

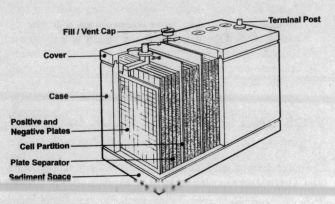

Art by Tim Kreger

## CLEANING YOUR BATTERY

Cleaning the battery is one of the most essential services that can be done on your car. It prevents power loss resulting from a dirty surface around the terminals or battery connections.

Dust and dirt are conductors of electricity, *especially when damp.* (Have you ever experienced battery problems during rainy weather?) You can have an invisible conductor of electricity on a dirty battery that slowly dissipates your battery's power. You probably won't see any sparks; however, there is a leakage of electricity. This could lead to a short. Here are the steps you should follow in keeping your battery clean:

1. Wear clothes you don't mind getting dirty. **Use eye protection and rubber gloves.** Battery acid touching your hands could cause serious burns. (If you contact the acid, wash your hands immediately.)
2. Remove the battery cables from the battery terminals. The battery cable clamps are removed by loosening the

nut on the clamp and moving the clamp back and forth until loose. I've seen some classic cars with the old spring-type clamp the prongs of which you'll have to squeeze with pliers to remove. You may find that battery acid has eaten away the cable clamp bolt and nut, making the nut difficult to remove. In this case, use a battery terminal puller found in most auto parts stores. When removing cables from the battery, inspect the condition of each of them at the clamp. If the insulation is deteriorated and you can see strands of wire, replace the cable at once.

**Note:** Always remove the ground-side cable first (this is usually the negative terminal); double-check your owner's manual just in case.

Removing the cables prevents an accidental spark from occurring if you happen to touch a metal part of the car with the pliers holding the cable. (See instructions for replacing cables later in this chapter.)

3. If your battery is of the old type to which you're still adding water, cover the holes in the battery caps with masking or electrical tape so your cleaning solution won't enter the battery. You don't need to take this precaution with the new sealed batteries.

4. I grew up cleaning batteries with baking soda and water, and a lot of folks still use this method. Mix baking soda with about a cup of water, using enough baking soda to fizz. Then brush the solution (I used an old toothbrush or paintbrush) on the top of the battery and rinse with enough water to clean all residue. Aerosols are now available that clean battery tops and terminals. These products do a nice job of cleaning, but are not as much fun!

5. Now that you have the clamps removed, you can begin cleaning the battery terminals. The old-fashioned way was to take a wire brush or steel wool and rub the terminals until clean. Now, of course, we have sprays that dissolve the corrosion that may build up on a battery terminal. Your parts store also carries a battery terminal cleaning tool, which will also do the job. Don't forget to clean the insides of cable clamps that contact the ter-

minals. This can be done with some sandpaper or by using the terminal cleaning tool, which generally converts to a clamp cleaner, as well.

6. You should now have a clean battery. Attach the cables back to the terminals in the opposite sequence that you removed them—i.e., attach the ground cable (usually negative) *last*. A note on attaching the clamps: I've seen a lot of shops actually pounding the clamps back on. The pounding is not necessary and could possibly damage the clamp or the battery itself. You can easily twist the clamps back on and tighten the nut.

## BATTERY CABLES

If you need to replace a battery cable because of cracked insulation allowing wires to show through, follow these steps:

1. **Get your safety glasses (to protect against flying debris) and rubber gloves back on!**
2. For whichever cable needs replacing, always remove the ground side first, in most cars the negative side. (Refer to above steps.) **Note:** The ground cable of the battery is identified by a negative symbol (-) next to the post on the top of the battery. Also, the negative cable is usually the color black and the negative post is usually the smaller of the two battery posts (on batteries with posts).
3. If you're replacing a negative cable, you're in for an easy task. Simply unbolt (in most cases) the end of the cable opposite from its position on the battery—usually inner fender or the engine block. Install the new cable as the old one came off.
4. To replace the other cable, which is the non-ground, usually positive, you'll have to follow that wire back to its connection. This is usually the starter motor solenoid. This may be a harder task because of the position of the starter. There is usually a nut to remove and replace with your new cable.

5. When re-installing cables, reverse the sequence as with removing cables and attach the grounded cable last.

## MISCELLANEOUS TIPS

Sometimes you can get by with only changing the battery cable clamp; however, with my cars and my customers' cars, I've always gone ahead and replaced the entire cable. I've found that if a clamp is that far gone, the cable is not far behind.

A couple other notes on battery maintenance:

- If your battery is the type that you check and add water to, only add distilled water or a good grade of drinking water.
- Never overfill a battery with water (fill to about an inch from the top).
- After attaching clean cables to clean terminals, apply a thin coat of petroleum jelly to protect against corrosion.
- Line the bottom of the battery box with a quarter-inch layer of baking soda. Doing so provides a cushion for the battery to rest on and absorption of any moisture that might collect in the air cavity between the box walls and the battery. More importantly, should your battery boil or leak acid, the baking soda will neutralize it before it can eat through the bottom of the box or even damage the car's frame.

## BATTERY TESTING

In testing a battery, there are two specific (and quite involved) procedures: One for batteries with removable filler caps and another test sequence for batteries that have a sealed top.

These tests require sophisticated and usually expensive equipment. You should leave this procedure up to your local technician. Your battery should be checked at least once a year, or before a long motoring vacation.

# JUMP-STARTING A BATTERY

Now, if you're stuck, how about a jump? Using the wrong procedure to jump-start a dead battery can result in a possible explosion, damage to the car's electrical system, or serious personal injury.

When attempting to jump-start a car, use good-quality cables and never attempt to jump-start a battery that has a cracked or damaged case.

Prior to jump-starting, make sure all battery cables are attached securely and beware of moving engine parts (e.g., fan, belts). Check the battery posts or connections for acid buildup, and clean them if necessary.

Because every car is different, the best way to learn about jump-starting a car is to read the owner's manual. The following jump-starting procedures apply to most cars:

1. **Wear safety glasses and insulated rubber gloves!**
2. Park cars close enough for jumper cables to be connected, but do not allow vehicles to touch. On both vehicles, put the transmission in park, or neutral for manual transmissions. Turn off engines and all electrical accessories. The power surge from a jump could destroy your radio, fan, phone, etc. Apply parking brakes.
3. Connect one end of the positive cable—usually red or marked with a plus (+) sign—to the positive terminal of the battery providing the jump. Connect the other end of the positive cable to the positive terminal of the dead battery.
4. Connect one end of the negative cable—usually black or marked with a negative (-) sign—to the negative terminal of the battery providing the jump.

5. Connect the other end of the negative cable to an un-painted, metallic surface—such as an engine bolt—on the car with the dead battery. Do not connect the negative cable to the negative terminal of the dead battery, because a spark will result that can ignite battery gases and cause an explosion.

6. Start the engine on the car providing the jump. When you attempt to start the disabled vehicle, follow the starting procedures outlined in the owner's manual and don't crank the starter for more than ten seconds. If it doesn't start, let the starter cool for two or three minutes before trying again.

7. Once the disabled car is running, disconnect the jumper cables in reverse order from which they were connected, last ones first, etc.

## SELECTING A NEW BATTERY

If you are in the market for a new battery, always select a replacement battery that has the same cold cranking amps (CCA) recommended by the vehicle manufacturer. CCA (0°F) is a long-established rating used to describe battery high-rate discharge capability at low temperature. It is the discharge load in amperes that a new, fully charged battery at 0°F (-18°C) can continuously deliver for thirty seconds. If you're installing your battery, refer to the safety considerations mentioned earlier in this chapter.

If you opt for a budget replacement that's not up to spec, you may run into problems with your charging system, starting system, or other electrical components. You can put in a battery rated higher than the original, but never go lower on the CCA rating. Don't settle for inexpensive jumper cables either. Select a quality set with at least a large, four-gauge copper cable.

## MOTORING TIP

## COLD WEATHER DRIVING

Fall and winter are hard on improperly maintained automobiles. Cold temperatures can increase wear on tires, belts, and hoses, render weak batteries useless, and cause inadequately protected engine cooling systems to freeze.

Motorists unfortunate enough to experience a winter breakdown can also find themselves facing life-threatening weather in addition to the dilemmas of unsafe or unfamiliar surroundings. This is the time of year you should plan on giving your vehicle a good winter checkup.

## PREPARATION

Here are some tips that I think everyone should follow when preparing for cold weather driving.

**Air Filter:** In cold weather a dirty or clogged air filter will do more to affect performance and fuel economy than in the summer months. Cold air is denser than warm air and is more dependent on a clean filter to flow efficiently into the carburetor or fuel injection system for complete combustion.

**Battery:** In freezing winter temperatures it can take up to five times more battery power to start a car than when the thermometer reads a mild 65 or 75 degrees. If the battery or any other part of the car's electrical system is in marginal shape, you'll have difficulty in cold weather. If your battery is more than three years old, the typical lifespan of most batteries, you're probably living on borrowed time. Have your technician or someone who specializes in auto electronics run a battery load test and check the complete electrical system, including the battery's reserve capacity. Replace severely corroded connectors. Have your voltage regulator checked, too.

**Cooling System:** Flush the system and fill with the antifreeze(coolant)/water mixture recommended by your owner's manual (a 50/50 solution is a good rule of thumb).

**Gasoline:** Always keep the gas tank as full as possible to minimize condensation, and prevent fuel contamination. Modern engines with fuel injection are especially fussy about getting their fill of clean gas.

**Ignition:** Wet weather can dampen an enthusiastic response from your car's engine, especially if it's an older car without electronic ignition. Worn points in the distributor, an old condenser, or a cracked distributor cap, combined with moisture, can make a car hard to start. And on cars of any age, frayed spark plug wires or dirty spark plugs will also cause starting problems.

**Starting:** Let your car warm up from one to two minutes before driving during freezing temperatures so the oil circulates to all moving parts.

**Tires:** On most new cars, all-season radial tires are standard equipment. They work well under most weather conditions. Check tire pressure once a week, especially in cold weather. Pressure can drop one pound per square inch (psi) for every ten degrees that the temperature drops. Remember, be sure your spare tire is also properly inflated.

**Windshield Wiper and Washers:** Check your wipers for proper functioning. Wiper blades that streak the windshield should be replaced. Worn-out wiper blades could also scratch your windshield. The washer reservoir bottle should be filled with an antifreeze washer solvent.

How about the wiper chatter you hear when your wipers are working? This is because of an oily film that develops on your windshield. To cure that problem, wipe your windshield down with rubbing alcohol.

Remember, the winter months are the hardest on your car, so take the time in the fall to get your vehicle into your technician.

# ON THE ROAD

Wintertime has traditionally made it difficult to navigate our highways. To help you avoid problems associated with driving during the winter months, you should follow my driving suggestions.

- Keep your speed down when driving on wet roads. Excessive speed is the major cause of accidents during the winter. Remember, the posted speed limits are for dry weather, not wet, slippery roads.
- Leave extra distance between your car and the vehicle in front of you. This will allow you the extra time necessary to respond to any situation. You'll also need more room to stop in case of an emergency (one car length for every 10 mph).
- If you're driving on a four (or more) lane highway that's wet, leave yourself an "out." Don't drive at the same speed right next to someone who may slide into you on a slippery road.
- Whenever possible, use low gears when driving downhill and around curves on wet roads.
- For stopping on ice and snow, lightly pump your brakes. This also applies to vehicles with antilock braking systems.
- To start on ice and snow, do it slowly for maximum traction and less wheel spinning. On very slick surfaces, start in second gear to prevent wheel spinning.
- If you're required to use chains, I would never drive over 25. Your chains, car body, and tires will remain in better shape if you drive at a lower speed.
- If you find yourself in a skid, don't brake heavily, don't jerk the steering wheel, and don't panic. Instead, turn your steering wheel *into* the direction of the skid and *gently* brake.

- When parking in freezing weather, avoid using the parking brake. The brake linings could freeze to the brake drum and disc. If necessary, block tires with rocks or other heavy objects.
- Use your seat belt every time you get in your car and insist on it for all passengers.

You should always carry with you an emergency kit while traveling in cold, snowy weather. Your kit should include:

- Tire chains (practice installing before you get into the snow)
- Small snow shovel
- Extra clothing (including hat)
- Work gloves
- Blanket
- Traction mats (floor mats will work)
- Ice scraper (plastic, not metal)
- Booster cables (good ones)
- Small bag of abrasive materials for traction (sand, salt, or kitty litter)
- Flashlight
- Cloth or roll of paper towels
- Fire extinguisher
- Warning devices—reflective triangles or battery-powered flashers

A final word on your cold-weather travel:

I've seen lots of folks who've driven through slush or been stuck in it complain later about a bad vibration in the vehicle. What happens is that mud, slush, or snow freezes to the inside surface of your wheels because of centrifugal force. At highway speeds, the additional weight throws the wheel balance way off and produces a vibration.

So, after you drive through slush, take a high-pressure water hose and clean the inside surface of your wheels as soon as you can. This will save you time and money trying to diagnose a strange, new vibration.

# LUBRICATION

□ □ □

Today it's more essential than ever to know how to get the most mileage out of your transportation, and proper lubrication is the key. In this chapter I'll discuss the following:

- Purpose of lubrication
- American Petroleum Institute (API) certification
- Grades of motor oil
- Checking oil level
- Driving conditions versus motor oil
- Oil changes
- Proper disposal of oil and oil filters
- Other lubrication

When you lift the hood of your car and contemplate all the parts connected to the basic engine block, you may wonder how it ever functions. And why it works so well for so long. Careful design is one reason, of course, but motor oil is what really adds to engine life. Motor oil is the lifeblood of your car's engine, keeping it clean and free from premature wear.

While your engine is running, oil coats vital parts to protect them from rust and corrosion. During engine start-up, there are intense, sudden stresses through the entire power plant. In some cases, contact between moving parts can amount to hundreds of thousands of pounds per square inch of pressure. And what makes the contact feasible is a quality motor oil with the ability to reduce friction and wear.

Motor oil seals tiny gaps between the piston rings and

cylinder walls. These gaps are easy escape routes for vapors and gases during the compression and explosion strokes. This coating of oil is very thin, but works well to prevent loss of power and operating economy.

What few people know is that a quality motor oil actually cools moving engine parts. In water- or air-cooled engines, only slightly more than half of the engine's cooling is done by water or air. The rest of the cooling, particularly in the lower engine block (rods, pistons, crankshaft, and camshaft if located there) is handled by motor oil that is circulating through the engine.

Motor oil cleans engine surfaces by holding foreign deposits (dirt, soot, ash, acid, and moisture) in suspension within the oil, away from engine parts, until the deposits are filtered or drained when the oil is changed. Your engine oil also prevents corrosion caused by chemical changes during engine operation. Just think, this oil is thin enough to allow the starter to crank the engine, and thick enough to provide complete engine protection—pretty amazing!

## API CERTIFICATION MARK

Regardless of the technical specifications, the motor oil you've been buying—even brand names—may not have met the minimum standards set by the manufacturer to maintain your vehicle's performance. Several studies and tests have documented the fact that substandard motor oils have made their way onto retailers' shelves, and possibly into your car's engine. An auditing system was required to help ensure consistency in meeting the minimum standards.

The American Automobile Manufacturers Association (AAMA), in cooperation with the American Petroleum Institute (API), has created a certification and licensing system that allows you to identify the quality of the oils recommended for use in your car or light truck.

*Valvoline Motor Oil. Used*
*with permission.*

Viscosity grade, fuel efficiency, and performance are all important and are covered by one mark—the API certification mark. The "starburst" symbol shown above is a direct result of AAMA's efforts in this area.

## WHAT'S THE BENEFIT?

Using API-certified motor oil helps maintain your vehicle's compliance with emissions standards. It can help lessen the likelihood of engine failure and extend the life of your engine. API-certified oils have been proven to meet auto manufacturers' standards for car and light truck gasoline engines.

Regardless of what brand of oil you always used, look for the API certified mark on the front of the next bottle of motor oil you buy. It's the best way to be sure that the oil you're putting into your car's engine belongs there.

## SINGLE-GRADE MOTOR OILS VERSUS MULTI-GRADE OILS

Single-grade oils (e.g., SAE 30, SAE 40) have temperature limitations—in very cold temperatures they will not flow easily:

- *SAE 5W,* for use where temperatures below zero are common.
- *SAE 10W,* for use in winter climates where temperature rarely gets below 0°F. Do not use above 60°F.
- *SAE 15W,* for use where temperature rarely gets below 10°F.
- *SAE 20W,* for use in areas that rarely get below 10°F.
- *SAE 30W,* for summer temperatures.
- *SAE 40/50,* for severe service, summer temperatures, towing, etc.

Even so, there are many engines that need single-grade oils. Check your owner's manual.

Multi-grade oils (e.g., SAE 5W-30, 10W-30) contain additives to enable the oils to perform in a wide range of temperatures. Adhere to owner's manual recommendations.

## CHECKING YOUR OIL LEVEL

1. Check oil level every other time you buy gasoline.
2. Check when engine is cold, parked on level ground.
3. Pull out dipstick, wipe with clean cloth.
4. Reinsert dipstick, then pull out and observe oil level.
5. Oil film should fall between "Add" and "Full" marks. (If the dipstick is not marked, see your owner's manual).
6. Never overfill or underfill your motor oil crankcase. (See your owner's manual for motor oil capacity.)

## OIL CHANGE FREQUENCY

- Consult your vehicle owner's manual.
- For maximum protection, I recommend changing oil every 3 months or 3,000 miles.
- Always change filter when changing oil.

# RECOMMENDED GRADES OF MOTOR OIL

- Consult your vehicle owner's manual.
- 5W-30 and 10W-30 are recommended by most domestic, European, and Japanese engine manufacturers.
- "Lighter" oils offer longer engine life, improved fuel economy, and better cold starting.

# DRIVING CONDITIONS THAT AFFECT MOTOR OIL PERFORMANCE AND CHANGE FREQUENCY

- *Severe service conditions,* such as towing, short trips, stop-and-go traffic, extreme heat or cold, and excessive dust or dirt, are very hard on motor oils and can cause oil additives to be depleted more quickly than high-speed operation over longer distances, leading to more frequent oil change intervals (every 2 months or 2,000 miles).
- *Normal service conditions,* such as long trips and highway driving are easier on motor oils (you could possibly go 5 or 6 months, 5,000 to 6,000 miles, if you're on the highway all the time).
- Consult your owner's manual for appropriate oil change intervals and consider the type of conditions under which you operate your car.

# MOTOR OIL CHANGE INSTRUCTIONS

1. Start your vehicle, letting the engine run 2 to 3 minutes, which allows the oil to heat up to normal temperature.
2. Stop engine.
3. Remove the plug from your oil pan.

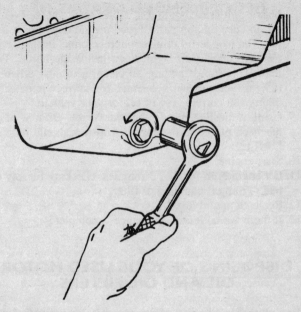

*Art by Tim Kreger*

4. Drain oil into a container so that you can take the used oil to a local recycling center.
5. Remove oil filter. Drain oil from filter into container for recycling. You may, if permissible in your state, dispose of oil filter in household trash. (Some states require that you recycle your filter.)
6. Place drain plug back in oil pan. Tighten. Do not over-tighten.
7. Replace used oil filter with new one, moistening the filter seal (gasket) with clean oil. Do not overtighten. Follow filter instructions.
8. Fill vehicle with required amount of oil. Here is a nifty way to put the oil into your car without creating a mess: When your family has used all the contents of a large

plastic soft drink bottle (the 2-liter size), cut the bottom off and use the top part (turned upside down) as a funnel. The wonderful thing about this funnel is that the oil can will usually fit right down inside the bottle. This makes the job of adding oil clean, neat, and efficient. (Check your owner's manual for correct number of quarts and correct type of oil for your vehicle.)

9. Using a dipstick, verify that the correct amount of oil has been placed in the engine. Dipstick should indicate "FULL."
10. Start engine.
11. Let engine run for 2 to 3 minutes, checking for any oil leaks from oil pan plug or filter.
12. Recheck the oil level.
13. If there are no leaks, oil change is complete.

# DISPOSING OF YOUR USED MOTOR OIL AND OIL FILTERS

Used oil that is disposed of improperly is a waste of a valuable energy resource and a threat to the environment. The oil from a single oil change can contaminate one million gallons of fresh water, a year's supply for fifty people. In 1992, the EPA reported that 60 percent of Americans change their own oil, generating between 200 and 250 million gallons of used oil per year. The EPA estimates that only 10 percent of do-it-yourself–generated oil is returned to collection programs for recycling or energy recovery.

Many who dump their oil on the ground or into storm drains, or throw it in the trash (all of which are illegal) simply lack the opportunity to take their oil to a convenient collection site for proper disposal. Be sure to ask your dealer or parts store where the closest location is to your home or office.

## THE DOS AND DON'TS OF USED OIL AND OIL FILTER RECYCLING

**Do** recycle used oil and used oil filters, because recycling protects the environment, saves energy, and conserves natural resources!

**Do** take used oil and oil filters to auto service centers, retailers, public recycling centers, or facilities that accept these materials for proper recycling.

**Don't** put used oil in the trash or pour it down the drain or sewer. Used oil is a serious pollutant to water resources. Just one gallon of oil can contaminate one million gallons of water.

**Don't** mix solvents, engine/parts cleaning fluids, or antifreeze with used oil. These fluid wastes will contaminate the used oil and may make it a hazardous waste rather than a recyclable material.

**Do** place used oil and used oil filters in clean, leakproof, and shatterproof containers for storage and transport to a recycling facility.

**Don't** put used oil in containers that contain potentially harmful residues, such as bleach, pesticides, antifreeze, or paint.

**Do** drop off used oil and oil filters at recycling centers only during business or operating hours, and follow their recycling instructions.

## A FINAL NOTE REGARDING MOTOR OIL

Some people think they can wait till the oil pressure light indicator or the oil gauge warns them that they need oil. *The truth is* that when this light comes on, or your dashboard gauge reads zero, *you are dangerously low on oil.* My recommendation is that you always keep a few cans of the same brand and weight oil in your car trunk for emergencies.

# OTHER LUBRICATION

The day may come when the good ol' lube job won't be necessary to keep our vehicles properly lubricated. Older vehicles with zerk or grease fittings at critical suspension points require regularly scheduled technician-applied lubrication. Components on today's cars receive special lubrication that should last nearly 100,000 miles before requiring attention.

There are specific areas on all cars that the owner needs to lube on a once-a-year basis (twice-a-year in damp, wet areas because the dampness washes away lubricant).

Dress the rubber moldings around the doors and treat the trunk seals with silicone aerosol. This will keep the rubber soft and pliable for a long time. Do not use any oil-based product on moldings or seals because of possible deterioration. For the door locks and hinges, you can use a penetrating oil like WD-40. Occasionally, squirt a lock lubricant or WD-40 into the slot where your key fits.

The wheel bearings are another area that requires regular service. Wheel bearings are "packed" with grease at the factory. As a result of the wheels' rotation, these bearings need to be removed, inspected, and repacked.

On most front wheel drive (FWD) cars, the rear wheels need to be packed; on rear wheel drive vehicles, the front wheels require packing (some FWD cars have sealed bearings in the rear that cannot be packed—see your owner's manual).

I would suggest that wheel bearings be packed every 10,000 miles for maximum bearing life, and remember, always consult your owner's manual and leave the job for your service technician.

# THE COOLING SYSTEM

❑ ❑ ❑

It gets mighty hot inside your automobile's engine—hot enough to actually melt the engine. To get rid of that heat and maintain the proper temperature, a cooling system is necessary. In this chapter we'll discuss

- Cooling system components
- Cooling system inspection
- Cooling system service
- Radiator hose replacement
- What to do when your car overheats

Unfortunately, many motorists wait until the first severe cold snap or the hottest day of the year before paying attention to their car's cooling system.

This often results in "crisis repairs" rather than preventive maintenance.

To understand your cooling system, let's look at the parts under the hood.

**Engine:** The engine consists of a block containing cylinders topped by a cylinder head with combustion chambers. An antifreeze/coolant solution works to diffuse engine heat so that the engine operates at the correct temperature for best performance and economy. In addition, the an-

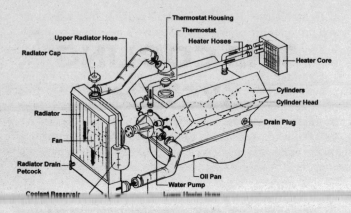

*Art by Tim Kreger*

tifreeze/coolant mixture protects the metal parts and water pump against the corrosion that occurs at high temperatures.

**Radiator:** Consists of a series of small tubes and fins surrounded by air passages that cool the mixture flowing through the radiator from the engine.

**Water Pump:** It pumps the coolant through the engine, radiator, and heater.

**Thermostat:** A temperature-operated valve that controls the amount of coolant that flows from the engine to the radiator. In cooler temperatures, when maximum cooling isn't necessary, the thermostat is almost shut. In warmer weather, the thermostat opens to allow enough coolant to pass through the radiator to maintain the normal operating temperature. If your engine runs too cold, as much damage can be done as if it runs at too high a temperature.

**Heater Hose:** Coolant flows to/from the engine to the heater core through this rubber hose. Corrosion particles can restrict these hoses, causing your system to function ineffectively. A proper mixture of coolant can help prevent this from occurring.

**Heater Core:** Basically a small radiator that warms air and provides the heat within a vehicle's passenger compartment. Like the radiator, the heater core is susceptible to corrosion and leaking.

**Cylinder Heads:** Does your car have aluminum engine components? If you don't know, it would be wise to find out. Aluminum heads are more vulnerable to damage from overheating than the traditional cast-iron type. Excessive heat can warp the temperature-sensitive heads, resulting in a major repair expense. It can happen so fast you may not even have other warnings that your car is in trouble.

## COOLING SYSTEM INSPECTION

The most common cause of overheating is loss of coolant due to an internal or external leak. Another culprit is a sticking thermostat, which prevents coolant from circulating through the engine.

To avoid the expense and inconvenience of trouble on the road, invest in an annual inspection of the cooling system. Overheating is a leading cause of mechanical breakdown.

### RADIATOR

Achieving more miles per gallon, a continuing challenge to automotive designers, has affected the cooling system as much as any part of the vehicle. To reach their objectives, engineers work to reduce wind resistance and vehicle weight, among other improvements.

These innovations have led to smaller radiators (to accommodate the reduced frontal area of the vehicle). And to reduce weight, the old copper and brass radiators with soldered joints were replaced with aluminum and plastic: lighter, less expensive, and with excellent life expectancy.

Aluminum, however, is more vulnerable to breakdown of the inhibitors in the antifreeze/coolant that protect against rust and corrosion. Failure to flush the cooling system and replace antifreeze/coolant can lead to the demise of a fairly new radiator.

Remember to flush those bugs, leaves, and other road debris from the front of your radiator with a brush and garden hose or an air hose if available. (Especially after a long trip.) These insects will affect air flow across your cooling system and cause your engine to run much hotter than normal and possibly overheat.

Finally, don't forget to inspect the radiator for leaks and corrosion, signs of impending problems.

## RADIATOR PRESSURE CAP

The radiator pressure cap serves as the safety valve in the cooling system. A good cap raises the boiling point of your cooling system inside the radiator for additional protection against overheating. **Remember, never remove a radiator cap when the engine is hot—NEVER, NEVER, NEVER—only check when cool and always remove cap slowly. Otherwise, you could be burned by the hot radiator water.**

Inspect the radiator cap. Replace it if the rubber gasket is broken, dried out, missing, or if you notice that coolant is leaking at the cap. You may also be in for a cap replacement soon if the cap can be removed easily. You should feel some friction when removing the cap.

A radiator pressure test, available at most service dealers, not only will disclose existing or potential leaks in the system, it also can detect a faulty pressure cap. This test should be done twice a year, spring and fall, before the two extreme temperature periods.

## RADIATOR HOSE

When one hose needs replacing, you're likely to find more in marginal condition. Rubber components under the hood live in a hostile environment, surviving temperatures ranging from sub-zero to more than 250°F. Hoses circulate as much as 7,500 gallons of coolant per hour at up to eighteen pounds of pressure.

Inspect radiator hoses for leaks, cracks, or soft, mushy condition. Tighten all clamps. Replace hoses as needed. (See "Belts, Chains and Hoses" chapter.)

## HEATER HOSE

Look for the heater hose running from the engine, through the firewall, to the heater core under the dash. Replace swollen or cracked hoses. To check the hoses, start the engine and turn on the heater. If after ten minutes the hoses are cool, they could be clogged.

## ENGINE BELTS

Inspect all engine belts for wear and cracks. Replace if worn, cracked, or glazed. Adjust loose belts.

**Note:** Some engines have a V-ribbed belt that drives some or all of the accessories. If the belt grooves show excessive cracks or "chunking," replace the belt. (See "Belts, Chains, and Hoses" chapter for a more detailed explanation of chunking and belts.)

## THERMOSTAT

Save gas with an efficient vehicle. Your car's engine, like your body, has an optimum operating temperature. Most engines run in the 195°–240°F range, controlled by the cooling system thermostat. But fuel economy drops 10 to 20 percent when engine operating temperature falls below 150°F. The small investment to replace a faulty thermostat can soon pay for itself, not only in gas savings but also in terms of reduced engine wear. Have it replaced every two or three years.

## CHECKING THE COOLANT

1. First determine if your engine has a coolant overflow recovery system. Again, your owner's manual will tell you.
2. If you have no such system, check coolant when the engine is cold.
3. Remove the radiator cap; the coolant should be about 1½ inches from the bottom of the filler neck.
4. If you have a coolant overflow system, check it when the engine is hot.
5. **Do not remove the radiator cap!**
6. Inspect the recovery reservoir, which should have "Full" and "Add" marks on its side. The level should be between these two marks. (Check your owner's manual for location of the reservoir.)
7. Check the condition of the coolant. If it is rust-colored, it should be changed. A correct color would be that of the coolant prior to being mixed with water and added to the radiator.

# HOW TO CLEAN, FLUSH, AND REFILL YOUR RADIATOR WITH ANTIFREEZE/COOLANT

To avoid problems resulting from rust, dirt, and mineral deposits in the cooling system, it's best to give your radiator an internal cleaning every year or two.

It's easy. Here's how to do it:

1. Start with a cold engine and the ignition off. Remove the radiator pressure cap.
2. Open or remove the drain plug at the bottom of the radiator and drain the coolant into a container.
3. Close the drain and fill the radiator with water.
4. Start the engine and turn the heater control to "Hot." Add a can of cooling system cleaner (radiator flush) to

the radiator inlet and let the engine idle for 30 minutes (or as per the instructions on container).

5. Stop the engine and allow it to cool for 5 minutes. Drain the system, as above.
6. Close the drain plug, fill the radiator with water, and let the engine idle for 5 more minutes.
7. Repeat step no. 5. Close the drain plug.
8. Install new 50/50 mixture of water and antifreeze/coolant.
9. Replace the radiator pressure cap.
10. Recheck the coolant level in a couple of days and add if necessary.

Many people mistakenly believe that they will have extra protection in extreme weather if they pour antifreeze/coolant into their car's radiator without thinning it with water as the manufacturer recommended.

More often than not, the proper ratio of coolant to water is 50/50; check your owner's manual to verify the ratio for your vehicle. What many people don't realize is that antifreeze/coolant concentrations higher than 50 percent can cause excessive water pump wear, possibly causing the pump to fail prematurely.

Now, if you're one of those people who tries to save money by using a higher percentage of water than recommended, the antifreeze/coolant won't provide the required corrosion, overheating, and freezing protection. So it's important not to try to save pennies here.

For those who are planning to head across country with ol' Betsy this year (or just across town), be sure to carefully select which coolant you use. If you have an aluminum engine, check to see if the coolant is compatible.

Some brands may contain less glycol, the main ingredient that protects against boiling and freezing. Always be sure that the coolant container has a seal and that the seal has not been broken. It's sad but true that some people have been ripped off by purchasing coolant that has already been diluted with water—look for a sealed container.

If you change antifreeze/coolant yourself, make sure it is disposed of properly. Many family pets have died after drinking from a sweet-tasting puddle of coolant.

The proper disposal method for used antifreeze/coolant is similar to that for used oil. Pour it into a heavy-duty container and take it to a disposal station or hazardous waste dump.


# REPLACING A RADIATOR HOSE

This should be done (depending on your climate) every three years or 30,000 miles. Tools required: screwdriver, crescent wrench, sharp knife, and pliers. Before starting, be sure the hose location is one that you can reach. If it's not, replacement may be a job for a professional.

Also, plan on installing new clamps. Old clamps are often rusted, or bent out of shape when they are removed.

1. Starting with a cool engine, remove radiator cap and open plug at bottom of radiator to drain coolant.
2. Remove hose clamps and discard. For easy hose removal, slit hose end, twist left and right, then pull straight off. (Do not force.)

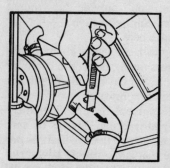 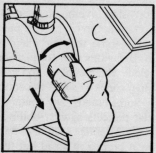

*Art by Tim Kreger*

3. Clean off outlets with clean cloth. Use sandpaper if necessary.
4. Dip ends of new hose into coolant for easier installation.
5. Install hose by pushing on—be sure hose covers full length of outlets.
6. Apply new clamps and tighten securely.
7. Add coolant and water as required.
8. Start engine and check clamped ends for leaks.

   **CAUTION: Keep hands away from all moving parts while engine is running.**

## IF YOU OVERHEAT ON THE ROAD

Cooling system failure has been shown to be the third leading cause of highway breakdown, behind running out of gas and tire failure. Maybe a reason for this is that we take our vehicle's hoses and drive belts for granted and we don't have them changed every three years or 30,000 miles.

If you see your car's temperature indicator light go on or if you see the temperature gauge climb into the red, pull over, stop, and turn off the engine. (If you're not able to escape a traffic jam and you're overheating, as uncomfortable as it may sound, turning the heater on high will help prevent the car from boiling over, by dissipating some of the heat.)

If you find a leaking hose or a hose clamp that needs tightening, attempt the repair after the engine has cooled down. **Remember, be extra careful working under the hood. Protect yourself against the heat and steam.**

You may not find any signs of a leak under the hood but you still must go to the nearest service facility.

If you can't find anyone experienced to help you, add water. **Never remove a radiator cap on a hot engine—you could be burned by the hot radiator water.** Here's what you should do: After you've had your engine off for at least fifteen minutes, start it up and drive for a short distance. Stop, cool it down for another fifteen minutes, and drive again for a short distance. By repeating this procedure until you can find help, you'll avoid major engine repair.

# MOTORING TIP

## TRAVEL TIPS

Now for the topic of readying your vehicle for the Great American Vacation. The following is my tried-and-true checklist to help make sure you travel safely:

1. Have your car safety checked and tuned up before you leave. You'll get better fuel economy and you'll have the ability to travel the interstates more safely because you'll have passing power when you need it.
2. Did you know summertime is the toughest on your battery? Excessively high temperatures accelerate certain chemical processes that speed deterioration inside the battery. This condition is aggravated by the high under-hood temperatures of newer cars. When you're not too sure about the condition of your battery, especially if it is more than a few years old, have it tested. And if you find it is in marginal condition, replace it before it lets you down out in the "sticks."
3. Get your oil, oil filter, and air filter changed (you should already be doing this every 3,000 miles). Remember, oil is the lifeblood of your vehicle, so you need to check the level frequently.
4. Test your brakes. A spongy feel, scraping noise, or pulling to one side are the first signs of problems. See a professional.
5. Check your cooling system. Flush and refill your radiator with coolant (antifreeze) every two years or 30,000 miles.
6. Inspect hoses and belts under the hood. Squeeze hoses—they should be pliable. Fan belts should be checked for deterioration. If hoses are hard or belts are frayed, replace them—but take your old hoses and belts along with you. They may come in handy if you break down out in the "sticks."

7. Inspect your air and gas filters. If necessary, replace them. They are inexpensive (most cars) and very important. In fact, I would change both filters before any long trip.

8. Check complete exhaust system for leaks.

9. Look at your tires—not only at the pressure, but at the way they're wearing. Tires should be rotated every 6,000 to 8,000 miles, including your spare tire (if possible). And remember, proper inflation can increase fuel economy.

10. Fill your windshield washer fluid reservoir with the correct fluid and install new wiper blades before a major trip. Don't forget window cleaner and paper towels for the road.

11. Check those head and brake lights. Take a walk around your car with them on. With the help of a friend, check your brake and turn signal lights.

12. Pack an emergency road kit, especially a flashlight. For safety reasons, I don't recommend flares. You should carry the following: first aid kit, jumper cables (good quality), tow rope with hooks, tire gauge, tire inflator (ask for one that is CFC-free and make sure it doesn't contain propane or isobutane; these chemicals may ignite from a spark and are very dangerous), extra coolant and water, emergency lights (flashers), freestanding reflectors, extra cans of oil, extra hoses and fan belts, fire extinguisher, a small set of tools, duct tape, an extra set of keys, fuses, a few quarters for phone calls or tolls, and a tarp, blanket, or something to lie on if you need to get under your car.

13. If you have to stop for service, remember that if your license plates identify you as a tourist you may be a target for an unscrupulous garage or mechanic. Stay with your car! Never sign a blank repair order, and always carefully review the repair order before signing. If you're given a questionable quote, search out a second opinion. I once heard of a woman who was told her car would not make it another hundred miles without extensive work. She chose to drive to the nearest Highway

Patrol office for another opinion. They looked at the car and were able to assure her that it would be just fine without the costly repairs.

14. If you need antifreeze/coolant while on the road (or in town), make sure the container still has the manufacturer's seal over the opening. This will insure that you won't get a bottle of watered-down coolant.

15. To avoid theft on your trip, don't leave valuables showing within your car. At night, park in lighted areas. To lock your steering wheel, turn it all the way to the left or right before locking the car.

Obviously, falling asleep while driving on a long trip can be deadly, so here are some tips on how to stay alert at the wheel.

1. Keep the car's inside temperature cool.

2. Keep your body involved while driving by not using your cruise control.

3. Watch your posture—keep your head up, shoulders back. Don't fully extend your legs. Instead flex them at a 45-degree angle.

4. Take frequent breaks. Stop at least every two hours and walk around (do bend-overs, etc—any exercise is valuable). Eat lightly.

5. Break the monotony by varying your speed level. If you're alone, talk to yourself. But don't think or talk about things that upset you.

6. If you smoke, don't! It can tire your eyes and deprive the car of oxygen. Chew gum instead.

7. If you get sleepy, a 20-minute nap should be enough to allow you to continue your drive safely.

If you follow my advice, you'll be assured of a safe and memorable motoring experience. So buckle up those seat belts, be sure you pick up the latest maps, and have a great vacation. Send me a postcard!

# AIR CONDITIONING

□ □ □

Have you had your car's air conditioner serviced lately? Get ready for a surprise if you haven't. Like so many things that have been affected by environmental concerns, air conditioning service is not the simple procedure it once was. Included in this chapter are

- Environmental concerns
- Air conditioning service
- The future for Freon
- Servicing tips

## OUR OZONE LAYER IN DANGER

The Clean Air Act is designed, among other things, to help protect the earth's ozone layer from the effects of escaping chlorofluorocarbons.

Scientists worldwide have concluded that chlorofluorocarbons (CFCs, also known by the trade name Freon) deplete the ozone layer. CFCs have been used in the manufacturing of many products, such as foam insulation, electronics equipment, refrigerators, and air conditioners, and are found in the common Freon used in auto air conditioning units. When allowed to escape, these chemicals drive some thirty miles above the earth to the stratospheric ozone layer—a layer of gas that screens us from the sun's powerful ultraviolet (UV-B) radiation. Once there, CFCs break apart—a process that releases chlorine, which then attacks ozone. A single chlorine atom can destroy more than 100,000 ozone molecules.

The ozone layer is being depleted over Antarctica (the so-called Antarctic ozone hole), but also to a much lesser extent over North America, Europe, and other populated areas. A depleted ozone layer allows more UV-B radiation to reach earth, harming human, animal, and plant life in many ways. Scientists around the world agree that increased UV-B radiation could over the long run cause a rise in cases of skin cancer and cataracts. Also, increased radiation could damage important food crops and marine ecosystems.

## AIR CONDITIONING SERVICE

The laws have changed the way air conditioning (a/c) service is done. Only licensed professionals are allowed to purchase R-12 refrigerant containers of any size. Recycling used refrigerant, with approved equipment, is required when completing a/c service or any other maintenance and repairs involving the removal of a/c hoses or components.

Professional refrigerant recovery and recycling equipment now allows technicians to remove Freon (containing CFCs) from vehicle a/c systems, recycle it for maximum performance, and reuse it. No longer will it escape into the atmosphere and damage the ozone layer.

Auto service shops now must use this type of equipment. So while you'll probably be able to have your air conditioning serviced at the same place you dealt with before, there will be a difference in the type and degree of servicing needed, and the cost.

The start-up cost for this new equipment can run between $5,000 – $6,000. All technicians who perform air conditioning service must be certified by attending formal training.

This is required for all shops servicing more than 100 a/c systems a year.

In the past, all that most shops did when you came in with an a/c system not blowing cold air, was to just add more Freon and send you on your way.

Service shops, for example, are forbidden from knowingly loading refrigerant into a leaky system, so more thorough maintenance is required. The bottom line result, a healthier environment and, as one might expect, a bit higher price tag for more thorough service, including more expensive materials and equipment.

## CFC/FREON PHASEOUT

All but the newest vehicles use CFC/Freon in their a/c units. The phaseout of the substance means that production will stop, but it does not mean that you have to stop using Freon or having your air conditioner serviced with it. The first important step for all vehicle owners with Freon-type air conditioners is to reduce unnecessary loss of refrigerant. Preventive maintenance, fixing leaks, and recycling at service are key actions to minimize the need for additional refrigerant after the phaseout of production.

But many vehicles with Freon air conditioners will require service past that date. What choices will these vehicle owners have? For vehicles under warranty, please consult your dealer. For vehicles not under warranty, you may have the choice either to continue to service your air conditioner with Freon or to have the vehicle modified to use the new safe refrigerant—R134a.

Even though there will be some Freon around after the initial phaseout, vehicle owners may decide that it makes more sense to have their air conditioning units modified to accept the alternative refrigerant. For example, if you are having major service performed on your Freon-type air conditioner, modifying the system to use R-134a may be appropriate.

Since the complexity and the cost of modifying a Freon system will vary by make and model of car, the decision to retrofit may make more sense for some vehicles than others. In many cases, retrofit of newer vehicles will require fewer changes and cost less than retrofit of older vehicles. Actual costs of modifying a system to accept an alternative may vary widely.

If you are considering the purchase of a new or used vehicle, ask if the air conditioner uses R134a, and if not, find out about any applicable warranties covering air conditioning service and repair. If you buy an extended warranty or service contract, make sure you find out whether it covers future air conditioning repairs or services.

## SERVICE TIPS

If you are not feeling any cold air coming out when you turn your air conditioning on, don't let just anyone say that your compressor is "out" and that you need another one. This is one of the most expensive parts of your a/c system—costing as much as $400 and up *just for parts* for most cars.

Your problem may be as simple as replacing a switch, relay, fuse, or drive belt. Have a qualified technician check your entire a/c system, and if it's determined that you really do need a compressor, I recommend a new one, not rebuilt. This is the only way to go and will save you money in the long run.

During the cold winter months, you'll run the risk of expensive repair down the road if you're not using your vehicle's air conditioner at least once a month.

The rubber seals inside the compressor, the hoses, and other components can actually deteriorate from lack of use.

The refrigerant, whether it's old-fashioned Freon or the new R134a non-CFC type, actually carries oil along with it during compressor use (air on). The oil circulates throughout the system and is vital for proper lubrication. A fifteen- to twenty-minute run at least once a month should be enough to keep your a/c in top condition and may be an additional safeguard toward protecting our atmosphere against harmful contaminants like Freon.

# THE FUEL SYSTEM

❑ ❑ ❑

Most cars on the road today have fuel injection systems that, literally, inject fuel into the engine. Conventional carbureted cars have a system that combines fuel and air in a precise mixture for all cylinders at once. In this chapter we'll discuss

- Fuel system purpose
- Air and fuel filters
- Air filter service
- Maintenance tips

The purpose of your car's fuel system is to bring the gasoline and air together in the correct proportions inside the carburetor or, in the case of fuel injection, just after the fuel injector. The carburetor or injector(s) is responsible for turning the gasoline into a fine mist and mixing it with air before it moves into the engine's intake manifold and then into the combustion chamber.

Fuel injection systems require less maintenance than cars equipped with carburetors. The consequence of a poorly maintained fuel injection system, however, is just as disastrous as the consequence of a poorly maintained carbureted engine, and, a lot of times, more costly to repair.

**I do not, however, recommend that you attempt to diagnose starting or driveability problems with regards to a computerized fuel system (carburetor or fuel injection).** Leave this work to a professional who has the experience and equipment to work on these emission control systems.

# AIR AND FUEL FILTERS

The presence of dirt or any foreign matter in your fuel system will sooner or later cause major problems. An engine needs the right combination of air and gasoline to run efficiently: About 10,000 gallons of air for each gallon of gas.

An air filter is a car's first line of defense against the outside world. Everything along the road—from dirt, dust, grit, and sand, to microscopic particles from other vehicles—spells potential disaster for your engine. An air filter has to stop these contaminants in their tracks and prevent them from causing serious damage to your engine.

If the air filter is dirty, it partially blocks the air flow, thereby upsetting the fuel-to-air ratio. This not only causes the engine to run poorly, it also increases fuel consumption and pollutes the air.

To check if the air filter is clogged:

1. Check your owner's manual for filter location.
2. Remove the filter per the steps outlined in your owner's manual.
3. Hold the beam of a flashlight behind and toward the filter.
4. If the light doesn't shine through, the filter should be replaced.
5. If it is necessary to install a new air filter, do so in the same way the old one came out.

How often you change filters depends on the area and climate you live in and how much you drive. But you should check the condition of your car's filter at least twice a year, more often if you live in a dusty or heavily polluted area.

A dirty fuel filter can cause an engine to act sluggish during acceleration or operation at high speeds. The filter also can be so clogged with contaminants that the engine will not operate.

Car makers today use some form of in-line fuel filter. Either a replaceable filter element is enclosed in a housing, or the entire unit, housing and element, is replaceable.

These simple routine maintenance tips can help prevent most fuel system problems:

- Change the fuel filter at 10,000 to 15,000 miles, or every major tune-up.
- The air filter and PCV (positive crankcase ventilation) valve should be checked every tune-up or at least twice a year.
- If fuel injectors need to be cleaned, it's best to let a professional shop do the job with a commercial cleaner.
- If you develop carburetor problems, never let anyone sell you a complete rebuild or a new carburetor without seeking a second opinion.
- Be sure to use a good quality fuel. Don't believe what you hear about high-octane fuel. If your engine doesn't require it, you will *not* notice any increase in performance from using high-octane fuel. You should only use it if your owner's manual says you should.
- If your engine "pings" on the fuel that it should use, high-octane may reduce the detonation (ping). You need to have your technician diagnose the problem first, however.
- When filling up at a service station, stop at the first click, never top off.
- If you happen to store your car for an extended time, say four to six months or so, it's best to keep the fuel tank full so no water or contamination will get into the fuel and rust out the tank.

# MOTORING TIP

## FUEL SAVING TIPS

When vacation times are right around the corner, expect to see higher fuel prices.

The way you use your vehicle and maintain it will have a significant impact on the amount of money you spend on fuel. Even if you own a fuel-efficient automobile, please pay close attention to my fuel saving tips.

- Be certain your car's cooling system is operating properly, including correct antifreeze level and mixture, as well as a correctly functioning thermostat. An engine that runs too hot causes excessive engine wear and reduces gas mileage. Extended engine warm-up or decreased engine operating temperatures can also waste gasoline.

- If your car has a V-8 engine, one misfiring spark plug can cut your gas mileage by 6 to 8 percent. If you have two plugs misfiring, your fuel economy could be reduced by 20 percent! (If you have a four-cylinder engine with only one plug bad, your mileage still drops by 20 percent).

- Your ignition timing, automatic choke, carburetor or fuel injector, and thermostat can waste gasoline if not adjusted according to factory specifications. This is especially important during the warm-up (when you're starting a cold engine). Excessively fast idle or a choke that sticks will dramatically reduce your miles per gallon.

- A professional diagnostic service could cover all components I've mentioned above. But also have your technician look at your air filter. A clogged, dirty air filter increases fuel consumption, causes increased air pollution, and can contaminate your engine oil. An out-of-tune vehicle can cut your fuel economy by 40 to 50 percent or more!

- Something only a few people think about—a tight-fitting gas cap—is essential to keep fuel evaporation from contaminating the air and wasting gas. So be sure to check that your gas cap fits properly. If it doesn't, replace it immediately to save fuel and our environment.

- Other offenders in contributing to poor fuel economy are—believe it, folks—your tires! I see many cars come into my shop with low tire pressure. It's ironic, since appropriate air pressure is the least expensive "fix," but if neglected it will cost money because of fuel economy loss and tire wear. Remember this: A drop of eight pounds in tire pressure can cause a 5 percent drop in gas mileage.

- Keep the front wheels in proper alignment. Avoid hitting the curb, and slow down on rough roads. Improper alignment not only causes faster tire wear but also puts an extra load on the engine and transmission, which, in turn, wastes fuel.

The *way* we drive can account for a big drop in fuel economy. Consider these examples.

- I've seen miles-per-gallon drop from seventeen to twelve (that's 30 percent) in one of my customer's cars. He drives just five miles per day, but always when the engine is cold. An engine is always more efficient when it's warmed up, so you need to consolidate your driving to take advantage of that. Cold engines only get two-thirds of the mileage they get when warm.

- Most vehicles get the best mileage at 35 to 45 mph. Newer, aerodynamic cars with more fuel-efficient engines and overdrive transmissions achieve their best economy at 50 to 55 mph. What's important to remember is that for every 5 mph increase over 55, most cars reduce their mileage by 1½ mpg simply due to wind resistance.

- Using the cruise control option on long road trips can save you up to 2 miles per gallon.
- Keep your windows rolled up while on the highway (use your air conditioner if necessary). Having your windows open at 55 miles per hour can cut fuel economy by 10 percent because of the increased wind drag.
- And I don't have to remind you that your air conditioner puts an extra load on your engine, resulting in increased fuel consumption. However, just try to turn off the air conditioner and use the air vents while driving in town during the summer months—impossible! But remember, if you're running on "gas fumes," you'll go a little farther with the a/c off.
- Don't carry any additional weight along with you if you're looking for that one extra mile per gallon. You'll use more gas when your trunk is loaded down.

Remember, if your car doesn't need premium fuel, don't buy it! Your automobile won't run any better, it'll just cost you more in the long run. (High-power-output performance vehicles usually require premium fuel.)

I get sick and tired of hearing gasoline companies talking about their high-octane premium gasolines that will help your car run better or perform better. What I can't understand is, if a high performance car like the V-8 Ford Mustang GT can run better on premium fuel, why wasn't its use specified in the owner's manual? The manual says it will run fine on regular unleaded, and it does! Folks, you're burning your money "out the exhaust pipe" by using high-octane gas in a car that only specifies a lower-octane regular.

A report in *Automotive News* said that the Federal Trade Commission got a major oil company to agree that its claims of more engine power and zip from its ultra brands were without "reliable scientific evidence." If the owner's manual doesn't call for premium, *don't use it!*

Worse still, a report from General Motors' R&D Center says that premium fuels are likely to cause higher hydrocarbon mass emissions.

Diligent car care and good driving habits can save you fuel and money. Practice my tips and you'll see a big difference.

# SECTION TWO

□ □ □

# OUTSIDE THE CAR

# THE LIGHTING SYSTEM

□ □ □

Driving after dark is tough enough without contending with visibility problems—non-working or incorrectly aimed headlights and other burned-out lights are a safety hazard. The period in which your lights are required, between the hours of 9:00 P.M. and 6:00 A.M., accounts for nearly 40 percent of all fatal traffic accidents. Research also shows that drivers see each other better during daylight hours with headlights on. (So use those low beams during the day, especially when traveling the interstates.)

So you can see how important it is for *all* of your vehicle lights to be in operation. In this chapter we'll discuss

- Checking the electrical fuses
- Replacing headlights
- Aiming headlights
- Directional indicators, taillights, brake lights, side marker lights.

The average car has forty-five lights, including instruments, dome lights, and so forth. Some cars have twice that many. How long has it been since you've taken a walk around your vehicle to be sure all of yours are working?

Automotive lighting systems include headlights, fog lights, turn signals, stop lights, parking lights, taillights, backup lights, side marker lights, instrument panel lights, and courtesy lights.

## CHECK THE FUSES

If a group of lights is out, such as parking lights, side marker lights, brake lights, or turn signals, you should first check your fuse box before attempting to replace the lighting units. Your fuse box location can be found by referring to your owner's manual.

A burned-out fuse is easily discovered. If the metal strip or wire extending from end to end is burned, resulting in two pieces, you need to replace the fuse.

Always replace the fuse with the exact amp replacement. Never go higher or lower. A higher-rated fuse as a replacement could actually cause component damage or possibly even a fire. Again, refer to your owner's manual regarding ampere/fuse specifications.

## REPLACING HEADLIGHTS

This is one of the easier tasks that can be performed by the home technician. When headlights go out, it usually means that you need to replace the light. First determine whether your lighting is through sealed beams or the latest composite headlights that come in a variety of shapes to fit the aerodynamic front ends of today's vehicles.

For sealed beams (which require the replacement of the entire lighting unit) follow these steps:

1. Remove the metal trim ring or cover.
2. The headlight retaining ring can now be removed. Round headlights are usually connected with three screws, but some rectangular sealed beams use four screws to hold in the unit. **Important:** Before you at-

tempt to loosen these screws, first locate the screws used to adjust the angle of the headlight beam. These screws should not be touched while removing the headlights. (Sealed beams usually have an aiming screw at the top or bottom and another screw at the right or left side.)

3. Once the headlight retaining ring is removed, the headlight will slide out of its housing.
4. Hold the headlight in one hand and grasp the wiring connector in the other, then gently pull the connector from the beam.
5. Inspect the connector for any corrosion (clean with electrical cleaner if necessary) and check that wires are not frayed or torn.
6. Install the new beam by pushing the connector fully onto the tabs on the back of the light.
7. Test new unit before you reinstall any rings or covers.
8. Position the new headlight properly into the mounting housing (beams are usually marked "Top" on lens).
9. Replace retaining ring, trim ring, and cover.

For composite lighting units, other than round or rectangular sealed beam units, you'll only have to change a burned-out bulb. Composite units are not secured by mounting screws and a retaining ring, as sealed beams units are. Follow these steps:

1. Open the front hood and pull out the wiring connector from the housing unit on the back of the sealed beam.
2. The connector is secured by either a plastic collar or a spring clip.
3. Either twist the collar counterclockwise or flip the spring clip to remove the connector and bulb.
4. Carefully remove the bulb from the connector. You may have to lift on a locking tap or slip a collar off the bulb.
5. **Important:** Never touch the glass portion of the new bulb that you're installing. Halogen bulbs are brighter than ordinary headlights and sensitive to the oil of your

skin. They will burn out prematurely because of an oil deposit left on the bulb. Handle these bulbs with tissue or gloves while positioning them into the connector and never touch a hot bulb.

6. Reinstall the connector and bulb into the unit and test the light.

# AIMING YOUR HEADLIGHTS

Improperly aimed headlights are common. High headlight aim can be due to an overloaded trunk, which can tilt the car upward and temporarily mis-aim the lights. This is a dangerous condition which can not only blind oncoming drivers, but also adversely affect your range of vision.

If you've replaced a headlight or if you're constantly being flashed by oncoming traffic, you may need to check your headlight aim.

## VEHICLES WITH BUBBLE-TYPE LEVELS

On some 1990 and later-model cars, you may find a simple way of checking and aiming your headlights. A bubble-type level sight-glass built into each headlight housing will check the setting. You'll need only to turn a screw after you've made sure your vehicle is on level ground. Refer to your owner's manual for specifics.

## VEHICLES WITHOUT BUBBLE-TYPE LEVELING DEVICES BUILT IN

For a simple quick-fix that's not 100 percent accurate, but close, follow these steps (see your technician for accurate headlight setting):

1. Pull your car up to a light-colored vertical wall or garage door with at least 25 feet of level ground clear in front.
2. Put a mark on the wall opposite the center of each head-light lens (with car close to wall, without lights on), two marks for two lights, four marks for four lights.
3. Move the vehicle 25 feet away from the wall.
4. Draw large, easily seen crosses through each mark made on the wall.
5. Turn on the low beams, check that the bulk of the light falls just below and to the right of the marks that corre-spond to the centers of these lights.

6. Turn the adjusting screws (you may have to remove a retaining/trim ring) in or out to move the beam as needed.

On two-light systems, setting the low beam will also set the high beam. On four-light systems, you'll have to repeat the above procedure with the high beam units.

You'll have to block out the low beams with a sheet of cardboard so you'll only see the high beams shining on the wall. The focus of the high beams should hit the wall at one to two inches below the center of the marks on the wall.

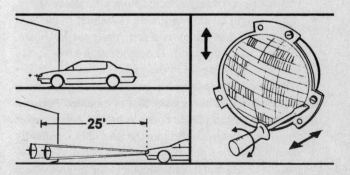

*Art by Tim Kreger*

After you've gone through the process, double-check your visibility adjustments by driving down a dark road.

## DIRECTIONAL INDICATORS, TAILLIGHTS, BRAKE LIGHTS, SIDE MARKER LIGHTS

To change these bulbs, you'll usually only need to remove an inside panel, then remove the bulb and connector, or just remove the connector to replace a bulb. On some lights you'll need to remove the lens covering the bulb. This is easy, however. Here are some tips:

- When buying replacement bulbs, match the number stamped on the base exactly. You'll find that bulbs with other stock numbers may fit, but will not always operate correctly and can cause electrical shorts or premature failure.
- When changing brake lights, running lights, and indicator lights, you'll have to touch the glass portion of the bulb. Because these are not halogen bulbs, they will not be adversely affected from your doing so.
- Apply a light coating of grease (Vaseline) to the base of the bulbs that you push in and turn to secure (brake, running, and indicators). This lubrication keeps corrosion from building up in the socket.
- When replacing lens covers on the above lights, check the condition of the gasket that is mounted between the amber or red plastic cover. A broken-down gasket could let moisture or dirt into the assembly, eventually shorting out the light. If the gasket is in bad shape, replace it or use household silicone in the groove where the lens fits. It provides a good seal.

# MOTORING TIP

## STORING YOUR CAR

As opposed to a vintage bottle of wine, the quality of an automobile in storage will not improve with age. Its value may go up, however, so there are certain precautions you must take to make sure your vehicle is adequately readied for storage.

A typical storage period is from six months to a year (about the time your college-age kids go to school). A car is always better off stored in a cool, dry place, preferably indoors.

Now to the nitty-gritty:

- The battery should be removed, but if it can't be taken out completely, at least disconnect the ground cable.
- As a pilot, I learned long ago that it's very important to fill the gas tank for the length of storage (up to one year) to keep condensation out of the tank. This prevents water damage or rust buildup.
- You should also have the engine oil and filter changed as close as possible to the time you put the car to bed—*drain the old oil out!*
- Remove the spark plugs and add about a teaspoon of new engine oil into each cylinder. Then reinstall the spark plugs. This will give the cylinders a protective coating.
- If any part of your engine is aluminum (block, heads, or manifold), drain the cooling system (radiator and engine block). This must be done to prevent any corrosion due to the coolant/aluminum contact. If your engine consists only of iron components, radiator coolant *should not be drained.* (If coolant is more than 1½ years old, drain and replace it.)
- Your brake system should have its fluid topped off. If the brake fluid is more than two years old, flush it. Old fluid will damage metal parts. And *don't* set the emergency brake.

- If you can, put your car on blocks or jack stands. This will ease the pressure on tires, bearings, and other suspension parts. What should you do if you don't have blocks or stands? Try adding 10 pounds more air to each tire.
- Cover the car with a good-quality car cover. Be sure the windows are cracked open just a bit for ventilation. This is true whether storing the automobile inside or outside.
- If you can, keep the car indoors. I've seen spiders, even rats, get into cars left outside (even under a cover). Those pesky critters can make nests behind the dash and even munch on rubber components and wiring.

For those of you currently keeping your "baby" under wraps: It may be spotless; however, how is it doing internally? It's not enough just to start it up, let it idle, turn it off, and put it back under the cover.

At start-up, your car is running rich, and this abundance of fuel contaminates the engine's oil. The car needs to be driven. As your speed builds up, so does the heat in the engine, and exhaust temperature reaches normal. The oil circulates through the transmission. Seals in the transmission will stay soft and pliable and oil will circulate around the differential gears. All of this happens when you take ol' Betsy out for a drive instead of just letting her idle in the driveway for a few minutes. For lubrication to do its job, it needs to circulate. This can only happen if you drive your treasured car for at least thirty minutes a week.

# THE TIRES

❏ ❏ ❏

Your vehicle's tires affect the safety, handling characteristics, performance, comfort, and cost of operating it more than any other component. Because they are the only part of the car that makes contact with the road, your tires deserve much more attention than most people realize.

This chapter includes the following:

- Tire wear versus the way you drive
- Tire inflation
- Tire tread depth
- Irregular tire wear
- Tire rotation
- Wheel balancing
- Wheel alignment
- Changing a tire
- Tire repairs
- Remounting wheels
- Replacing tires

## DRIVING HABITS

To increase the life of your tires you must avoid bad driving habits such as

- Fast starts and panic stops
- Fast turns on curves and around corners

- Riding on the edge of the pavement, driving over curbs, chuckholes, or other obstructions.

Aggressive driving (jackrabbit starts, "screeching stops," and "squealing turns") leads to abrasive tread wear and generates additional stress in tire sidewalls and shoulders. These can lead to premature wear or failure of the tire.

Road hazards are a leading cause of premature tire wear. Driving over road debris or obstacles, or hitting curbs, can cause severe tire damage. This damage may be visible from cuts or tears in the sidewall or tread, or may be hidden internal damage which can cause problems later.

In addition, hitting road hazards can jar suspension and steering components out of alignment. This misalignment may lead to the tire wear discussed previously.

## TIRE INFLATION

Properly maintaining your tires is a relatively simple task that can save you money and headaches down the road.

Tire life decreases about 10 percent for every 10 percent the tire is underinflated. In fact, an average passenger car tire could lose about one-third of its life at 20 psi (pounds per square inch), according to the Goodyear Tire and Rubber Company. Twenty percent of every dollar spent on tire replacement is a direct result of underinflation and overinflation.

The National Highway Traffic Safety Administration also estimates that about 250,000 accidents a year result from improperly inflated tires.

You should get into a practice of checking your tire pressure at least once a month (most people who drive for a profession should check pressure every *two* weeks). *Always* check pressure before a long trip.

To find the correct inflation pressure for your tire, look for a sticker on your vehicle's door post or glove box door,

*Art by Tim Kreger*

or in your owner's manual. Be sure to check the air pressure when tires are "cold" (i.e., driven less than a mile after being stopped for at least three hours).

Never "bleed" or reduce tire pressure when tires are hot. A tire's air pressure will automatically increase as its internal temperature increases. This increase is normal and should not be adjusted.

Tire pressure should be increased when your car is carrying extra weight, such as on a vacation trip. An increase of 4 psi over the car manufacturer's recommended cold-tire pressure is usually adequate.

I suggest that you not rely on your service station's air gauges. Some air pressure towers at service stations are inaccurate because of exposure and abuse. Invest in a decent tire gauge and don't forget to check the pressure in your spare tire (something that we check at my shop during every service).

If your tires lose more than four pounds pressure per month, the tire, the valve, or the wheel may be damaged.

# CHECKING TIRE TREAD DEPTH

Each time you check the tire pressure, take a look at the tread. Tires with less than one-sixteenth of an inch are considered bald and should be replaced.

Here's an easy way to test to see if the tread on your tires is dangerously thin and that it is therefore time to replace the tires on your vehicle (whatever you drive).

Take a Lincoln penny (head at top) and stick it between the tread of the tire (into the groove). Now, if the tread on your tires is OK you shouldn't be able to see the entire face of Mr. Lincoln on the penny. If the entire face is showing, then it's time for you to start shopping for replacement tires.

# IRREGULAR TIRE WEAR

By learning to read the early warning signs, motorists can prevent wear problems that shorten tire life by thousands of miles.

Underinflated

Tires give signs of problems in plenty of time to have them fixed, say the tire experts at Goodyear.

The most common signs of tire problems are under- and overinflation, feathering, one-sided wear, and cupping. Underinflation causes the most trouble of all because motorists usually don't check their tires as often as they should.

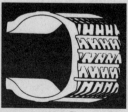
Overinflated

When a tire is underinflated, most of its contact with the road is on the outer tread ribs, causing them to wear faster than the middle of the tire.

With overinflation, the opposite wear pattern appears: The center tread gets more than its share of action with the road and it wears much faster than the outer ribs.

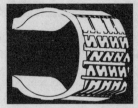

Feathering

Feathering—a condition where edges of the tread ribs take on the appearance of feathers—is caused by erratic scrubbing against the road when a tire is in need of toe-in or toe-out alignment correction.

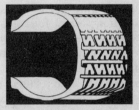

Excessive Camber

When an outer rib or the shoulder of a tire wears down faster than the rest of the tire, it is the sign of another type of alignment problem—excessive camber, which means the tire is leaning too much to the inside or the outside of the tread, making the tire work more on one side or the other.

Cupping

Cupping—when dips or cups appear in the tread—may be a sign wheels are out of balance or that shock absorbers and ball joints are worn.

*Goodyear Tires. Used with permission.*

If you find any irregular tire wear patterns, have them corrected immediately. It's a lot cheaper than a new set of tires.

# TIRE ROTATION

The process of tire rotation places the tire and wheel at a predetermined new position on the car.

By rotating your tires every 6,000 to 8,000 miles you'll get up to 20 percent longer tire life, and possibly more if you're using the spare tire in rotation. Tire rotation can also minimize irregular or uneven wear caused by maintaining a tire in one position over an extended period. If you have a normal-sized spare tire, get it into the rotation plan also. The rotation should follow a cross-rotation plan. That is, the spare should go to the right rear, right rear to the right front, right front to the left rear, left rear to the left front and left front to spare. With directional tires (tires specified by the manufacturer to rotate in only one direction for high performance), you can only rotate on the same side of the vehicle.

# WHEEL BALANCING

Out-of-balance wheels can also rob tires of thousands of miles. For a tire to run true, the weight of the tire and wheel assembly must be distributed equally. Improper balance can lead to "cupping" and excessive wear of the tread at the heavy spot.

Tire and wheel assemblies can be balanced in two ways: statically and dynamically.

Static balance is also called single plane balance. Tires are statically balanced when they are done on a bubble balancer. When an out-of-balance tire and wheel are mounted on a freely moving spindle, any heavy spot rotates to the bottom. Weights are added to counterbalance the heavy spot. Once the heavy spot has been balanced out, the tire stays at any position it is placed on the spindle.

Dynamic (two plane) balancing reveals whether a tire/wheel assembly is unbalanced from side to side as well as about its center. Dynamic imbalance can result in vibration and, sometimes, a steering wheel sensation called shimmy (where the wheel moves side to side in your hands).

Most modern tire service locations use off-the-car computer balancers for both static (single plane) and dynamic (two plane) balancing.

**Note:** Radial tires should always be dynamically balanced.

Tires and wheels should be balanced
- When new tires are mounted on wheels for the first time.
- When tires and wheels are rotated.
- When used tires are mounted on existing wheels.
- After flat repair.
- Any other time a tire is dismounted and remounted.

Balance should also be checked at the first sign of vibration, shimmy, or unusual tread wear. Any noticeable vibration or irregular tread wear should be taken to a professional for diagnosis.

# WHEEL ALIGNMENT

To get maximum life out of your set of tires, you should also have the wheel alignment checked regularly.

A vehicle is said to be properly aligned when all suspension and steering components are sound, and when the tire and wheel assemblies are geometrically set to run straight and true.

Automotive suspension systems involve moving parts, so wear of steering and suspension components is normal and is expected. As these components wear, however, alignment changes and it has to be adjusted to bring the settings back into the specification range.

Alignment is also sensitive to ride height. As the springs get old and sag, or suspension bushings deform over time, the vehicle rides lower and misalignment occurs. This changes the load distribution across the tire and affects the rate of tread wear (i.e., a heavily loaded area will wear more quickly than a lightly loaded area).

Whatever the cause of misalignment, the result is that the tires do not roll as straight as they should. This causes scuffing, uneven, rapid tread wear, and a loss of fuel economy.

One bad pothole can misalign or damage the suspension system. Considering the condition of our roads, it would be a good idea to have your alignment checked at your next service. Have your technician pay special attention to your shocks or struts, bushings, wheel bearings, ball joints, and steering system.

For a more detailed explanation on wheel alignment see the "Suspension and Steering System" chapter.

## HOW TO CHANGE A TIRE

1. Make sure the engine is off, the emergency brake is on, and the flashers are flashing.
2. Open the trunk and remove the spare tire, the jack, and the jack handle.
3. Put the jack under the jacking point of the car (check the owner's manual for location).
4. Jack up the car just enough to take the weight off the tire.
5. Remove the hubcap with a jack handle.
6. Loosen the lug nuts one full turn with the lug wrench (most cars' lug nuts go counterclockwise).
7. Jack up the car more so the tire is loose.
8. Remove the lug nuts and keep them on the hubcap so they don't get lost. Be sure to protect the outside of the hubcap from scratching.
9. Remove the tire.
10. Put the new tire on.

11. Put the lug nuts back and tighten slightly.
12. Let the car down so the weight is on the tire.
13. Secure the lug nuts.
14. Lower the jack all the way.


## HAVING A TIRE REPAIRED

If you have a flat tire repaired, don't assume that it's been done properly. A lot of service stations and shops across the country still insist on plugging a flat tire instead of removing the tire from the wheel and sealing the tire with a patch from the inside. When a plug is used, the technician must first enlarge the hole to get the plug in place. I've seen plugged tires later develop cord separation, where water can enter the tire through the plugged area.

Also remember that tires are to be patched only in the thread area, not in the sidewall. A tire with a sidewall problem or puncture should be replaced.


## CORRECTLY REMOUNTING WHEELS

Did you know the most common way of remounting wheels after alignment, brake, or tire work could also be the most damaging?

Air-impact wrenches are commonly used for this purpose at service stations and garages, to "zip" a wheel back up against a hub. Final tightening should *always* be done with a torque wrench.

While impact wrenches save time and effort *removing* lug nuts, they should **never** be used to tighten wheel lug nuts because the amount of torque applied can vary from nut to nut and car to car. This causes uneven loading on both the wheel and the hub. The uneven torque can also distort the brake

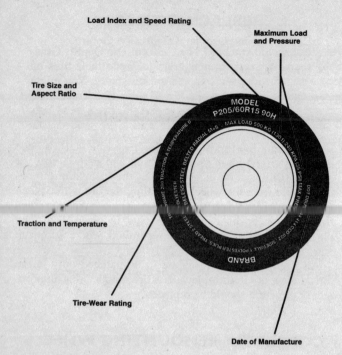

Load Index and Speed Rating

Maximum Load
and Pressure

Tire Size and
Aspect Ratio

MODEL
P205/60R15 90H

MAX LOAD 590 KG (130 1) 240 KPA (35) PSI) MAX PRE

Traction and Temperature

BRAND

Tire-Wear Rating

Date of Manufacture

*Art by Tim Kreger*

rotor and/or brake drum, causing a pedal pulsation to develop.

When a wheel is overtightened, besides the possibility of
cracked bolt holes, stripped nuts, or broken studs, you'll find
it very difficult to remove the wheel by hand in a roadside
emergency. You should know the wheel torque specs on
your vehicle and insist that your wheels are tightened with a
torque wrench to the manufacturers' specification.

# REPLACING TIRES

Which tire should you buy? The Uniform Tire Quality Grading System requires manufacturers to grade their tires on tread wear, traction, and temperature resistance. You might see this on the tire's sidewall: "Tread wear 120, Traction A, Temperature B." This would mean that this tire's tread lasts 20 percent longer on a test course than a tire graded 100. Traction grades A, B, and C, from best to worst, reflect the tire's ability to stop on wet pavement (under controlled conditions). Temperature grades A, B, and C, rate the tire's ability to dissipate heat; sustained high temperatures increase tire wear.

Never choose a tire smaller than the size that came with the car. Smaller tires may not be able to support the loaded weight of the vehicle. Tires should always be replaced with the same size designation—or one of the approved options—recommended by the auto or tire manufacturer.

# INTERIOR AND EXTERIOR CLEANING

□ □ □

We're all proud of our vehicles when they're in tip-top shape. It just feels great to be in a clean car. And it goes without saying that a car will be more valuable if its appearance has been well maintained—possibly twice as much as a neglected one at trade-in time. Dealers like a car that requires minimum repairs before being put on the market. In this chapter we'll discuss

- Washing and waxing your car
- Wheel cleaning
- Vinyl top cleaning
- Dents and scratches
- Road trips
- Rust
- Interior care

## EXTERIOR

Keep up with your touch-up work. Nicks, scratches, and "parking lot dents" ruin your vehicle's appearance and its value. Regular washing and seasonal cleaning and waxing can add years to the life of a paint job.

For years the cleaner of choice for many of us has been dish-washing liquid or other household detergent, which is handy and relatively inexpensive. However, these products often are far too concentrated. On newer cars the clear-coat finish can be dulled with improper washing with the wrong cleaner or wax. Most manufacturers of car cleaning products, like the folks at Meguiar's, Inc., offer special products for washing, cleaning, and protecting a vehicle exterior with the new finishes.

## WASHING YOUR CAR

1. Never wash your car in direct sunlight or wash a car when the surface is hot.
2. If possible, use a large, five-gallon, bucket for your water and car wash solution. This size container will allow the dirt to settle to the bottom and not be caught up in your cloth.
3. Hose down entire car to float loose dirt away.
4. If you need to use a cleaner for tree sap or road tar, do it at this time and rinse the area immediately.
5. Working on a wet car, use a car washing mitt or soft cotton cloth and apply your car wash solution to the car working from the top down and rinsing frequently.
6. To dry, use white, soft towels for best results.

## WAXING

Most manufacturers offer an array of cleaners, polishes, and waxes for consumers and professionals, and provide basic instructions on usage to avoid any confusion.

To remove defects, choose the least abrasive cleaning product available, depending on the seriousness of the problem. For example, a more abrasive cleaner should be used for deep scratches and severe acid rain stains than for mild oxidation or water spotting. By choosing the least abrasive product, you will spare the clear coat, which is very thin, any unnecessary deterioration.

Using proper techniques will not only save time, but will help guard the finish against damage. Always use a foam polishing pad or a 100 percent cotton terry-cloth towel when applying cleaners and polishes, to avoid scratching. When removing more serious defects, use an orbital or rotary buffer. Buffers will do much of the work and will also remove heavier defects, which are often impossible to eliminate by hand. Work on one small section at a time. Move the buffer or towel consistently, without excess pressure, using overlapping strokes. To avoid heat buildup and friction, never buff until the surface is dry.

Using the same buffing techniques, follow the cleaning step with a pure polish to provide the finish with oils and nutrients and to restore luster. When changing products, always use a separate buffing pad and **never** mix a cleaner and a polish on the same pad.

After the defect is removed and high gloss is restored, protect the finish with an application of premium Carnauba wax.

## BRAKE DUST

Along with winter muck, tires and wheels also get covered with brake dust. This black dust, prevalent with the new non-asbestos disc brake pads, can be difficult to wash away. New products made specifically for wheel and tire cleaning speed the cleanup process without damaging the bright finish on wheels.

## CAR TOP

Your car's vinyl top is at risk if you apply the wrong product. Many owners make the mistake of using interior cleaners on the vinyl top. Although this mistake is not permanent, applying the right product the first time will save elbow grease, money, and possibly, your top.

## DENTS, SCRATCHES

If you've encountered a small-to-medium-sized dent, try this: Take a large bathroom toilet plunger and center the rubber suction cup over the dent. Now push in as far as possible to get the maximum suction and *pull* the plunger off fast. Hopefully the dent will disappear at the same time. (Sometimes it helps to have the plunger cup wet, and make sure the car surface is clean.)

It doesn't always work, but when it does work, you amaze your friends and save a lot of money to boot.

For paint touch-ups, use the torn edge of a match from a book of matches as a brush. This enables you to dab a very small amount of paint into the chipped area so that you're not left with an unsightly blob of paint. And, to prevent rust, repair minor dings and scratches as soon as possible.

## ROAD TRIPS

After a road trip, especially during the summer months, make sure you clean the bugs and low-flying animal droppings from your paint. Acid from insect bodies can damage the paint, especially if left on for days, when the sun has a chance to "cook" this acid into the finish.

# RUST

Rust is a major problem in certain parts of the country. The most important thing I did to my vehicles when I lived in a "rust belt" was to visit the car wash frequently and to thoroughly wash the underside of the car. Once I saw rust develop, I cleaned the area a.s.a.p. I've also had limited success treating the area affected with a clear silicone sealant (in the tube).

# THE INTERIOR

Many of us spend more time in our cars than we do in our living rooms. So why shouldn't the furniture, carpeting, and ceiling of the second "living room" get its share of attention? Good car-keeping improves driving pleasure and safety, and increases the value of your vehicle.

As with the outside of your car, there are certain materials that are specifically recommended for the interior. For example, you want a vinyl upholstery cleaner that not only cleans but also protects the material from cracking. And you may need fabric and carpet cleaners designed to attack the specific stains in your car. There are two basic types of stains: protein (as from food spills) and oil/grease. Protein stains demand an enzyme pretreatment, while the oil/grease type can be removed with a heavy-duty shampoo containing degreasing agents. Be sure to give these chemicals time to work and remember always to work a stain from the outside in. Floor mats can be cleaned in the same way, finishing with a good shampoo.

## OTHER INTERIOR CLEANING TIPS

- Periodically clean door panels, upholstery, carpeting, and dash. All fabrics last longer when they're cleaned and given a protective treatment.

- I've cleaned vinyl interiors with a teaspoon of Murphy's Oil soap added to a quart or so of warm water. It does a wonderful job and doesn't leave an oily film.
- Common petroleum jelly has worked wonders on dry, faded vinyl. First, allow the area (to be treated) to warm up. (A car left in the sun on a 70-degree day for thirty minutes.) Apply the jelly, let soak into the vinyl for fifteen minutes, then buff. You'll be amazed with the results.
- Use a small paintbrush as an interior detailing brush. It's an inexpensive tool for cleaning dust out of nooks and crannies. Q-tips also work great on the interior.
- Repair or replace worn or damaged parts like sun visors, padded dash, door panels. As a cut or tear grows, so does the repair bill.
- Why put up with a torn or sagging headliner? Not only is this unsightly, it can also obstruct vision. New padded headliners are readily available, inexpensive to replace.
  **Note:** Heat can loosen the headliner. Prevent further damage by keeping windows cracked in hot weather.
- The floor covering in your car, truck, or van takes a lot more punishment than carpeting in your home. For a fresh look, replace worn carpeting.
  **Warning:** Don't take chances with a hole worn in the carpeting below the accelerator pedal. It can catch a heel when braking.
- Just as body dents and scratches grow worse with age, so do tears and worn spots on seat upholstery. Literally, a stitch in time can save complete replacement of upholstery and padding.
- How are your seat belts? Is the fabric strong enough to save you in a collision?
  **REMEMBER: Worn, damaged seat belts should be replaced.**

At an average price of more than $22,000, today's cars represent a major expenditure for most families, an invest-

ment that deserves better care than most vehicles ever receive.

Make a special effort to protect that investment. It will
pay off not only at trade-in time but during the years you're
enjoying your vehicle.

# MOTORING TIP

## WINDSHIELD WIPER AND WASHER CARE

A couple of the most overlooked areas of a vehicle are the windshield wiper blades and washer reservoir. Unfortunately, we often discover too late that we needed to replace those wiper blades, when driving behind a "big rig" during a rainstorm. Or we'll discover while traveling cross-country that we should have filled up that washer bottle. Keeping a close eye on your windshield wiper system is as important a safety measure as having headlights that work properly.

The common windshield wiper unit is composed of three parts:

- The wiper blade frame, which holds the rubber wiper that contacts the windshield. The frame is made of either metal or plastic.
- The rubber wiper blade, which does the work of cleaning the windshield. This is a refill that slides into the wiper blade frame.
- The wiper arm, which is designed to press the wiper against the windshield. These arms are usually made of metal.

## REPLACING WIPER BLADES

1. For maximum visibility, change wiper blades every 6 months. Refills are sold by the inch; measure your blade before you buy.
2. The blade refill slides out of the blade frame.
3. To release the old blade, either push the release button, usually red in color, or squeeze the two small metal tabs together located at the end of the frame.

4. The blade slides into place the same way the old blade came out.
5. Be sure to lock the refill back in the frame (with a click of the release button or metal tabs.)

## WINDSHIELD WASHER CARE

Most cars have a reservoir to hold washer fluid. This washer comes in handy, if your windshield is unexpectedly covered by dirt while driving. Most folks just add water; however, I'd recommend special windshield washer fluid, either ready-mixed or in concentrate form.

This special fluid cleans a lot better than water, and in wintertime it acts as an antifreeze. This will prevent a frozen washer system during inclement weather.

## WINDSHIELD CARE TIPS

- To keep your windshield free of that oily film and to keep your wipers from "chattering," wipe the glass down with rubbing alcohol.
- If your windshield wiper motor fails, this trick should keep the windshield clear: Cut a potato in half and rub it on the windshield. Rainwater will then bead off, so you'll be able to see. Then get the wiper motor repaired as soon as possible.

# SECTION THREE

□ □ □

# UNDERNEATH THE CAR

1. FRAME MEMBER
2. STABILIZER
3. DISC BRAKE
4. DISC BRAKE CALIPER
5. STEERING TIE ROD
6. EXHAUST SYSTEM
7. TRANSMISSION
8. CROSSMEMBER
9. CATALYTIC CONVERTER
10. EXHAUST RESONATOR
11. UNIVERSAL JOINT
12. DRIVE SHAFT
13. DIFFERENTIAL
14. REAR AXLE
15. FUEL FILL TUBE
16. MUFFLER
17. TAILPIPE
18. REAR FRAME MEMBER
19. FUEL TANK
20. LEAF SPRING
21. SHOCK ABSORBER
22. FRONT SUSPENSION AND STRUT
23. RADIATOR

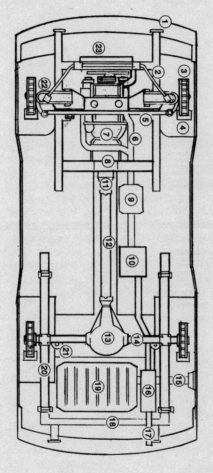

# THE EXHAUST SYSTEM

□ □ □

The exhaust system is one area of a car that, if ignored, could be hazardous to the occupants of any vehicle. An exhaust system that is maintained properly will keep the driving noise down and the passengers alive. In this chapter we'll discuss

- Exhaust system inspection
- Rust and vibration
- Emission system
- Exhaust fumes
- Parts

The exhaust system is basically the conduit that carries burned gases from the engine to the rear of the car. Once they are safely past the passenger compartment, the burned exhaust gases are released to the outside air.

There are a number of reasons for keeping your exhaust system in good condition. The most important is that a well-maintained system prevents dangerous carbon monoxide gas from entering the passenger compartment.

There has been a trend by automakers toward the use of stainless steel exhaust components. High-temperature stainless steel doesn't have the corrosion problems common with ordinary cold rolled steel; however, it is more brittle and more susceptible to fatigue breakage.

# INSPECTION

A routine check of your exhaust system, even if it is stainless steel, is one of the most important safety measures you can take. The best way to check your entire exhaust system is to have your technician raise your vehicle on a service lift. Unfortunately, this is not always convenient, so here are steps you can follow to inspect an exhaust system with a set of drive-up ramps in your driveway.

1. With your engine idling, slowly move around your car, preferably close to the ground, listening for any hissing or rumbling sounds that might indicate leaking connection points or breaks in the pipes or muffler. It should be easy to locate the source of a leak, but **BE CAREFUL, the exhaust system is hot and could burn your face or hands.**

2. Next, for your visual inspection, look at every part of the exhaust system, from your exhaust manifolds (which take the exhaust out of the engine—where exhaust piping begins) through the exhaust tip at the rear of your vehicle. A flashlight and screwdriver will be helpful in locating holes, cracks, or excessive rusting. A bent or kinked pipe could result in excessive back pressure, poor fuel economy and performance, and engine damage.

3. Inspect each pipe connection to see that all clamps are tight. Check for loose connections at the muffler by pushing up on the muffler. **(Caution: Make sure vehicle and exhaust system are cold.)** White, powdery deposits may indicate that a connection is loose or that the gaskets (at the exhaust manifold) are leaking.

4. With a screwdriver, tap the tailpipes and muffler to hear whether your components are in good shape. You should hear a solid metallic clink, which means the part is still good. A "thud" sound indicates a part that has started to deteriorate, which you may need to replace

soon. A rattle sound also indicates a part that may need replacing.

## RUST AND VIBRATION

I have seen and worked on thousands of exhaust systems during my "thirty-five years on Third Street in Los Angeles." And the major enemies of your car's exhaust system are rust and vibration.

It's interesting that the rust, which will eventually destroy a muffler or other components, develops on the *inside* of the part, not the outside. This is a by-product of stop-and-go driving. It's the constant heating up and cooling down inside pipes and mufflers that causes this rust.

You can also easily tear up an exhaust system with constant vibration from a worn-out suspension system. The hangers that support exhaust components can't take that type of constant jolting. I've seen a bad suspension literally tear apart an expensive new exhaust system. You'll also notice that as your car ages it becomes noisier as a result of exhaust part deterioration from the high exhaust temperature.

## EXHAUST EMISSION SYSTEM

On vehicles manufactured after 1975, a catalytic converter is a required component of the exhaust system. This is a stainless steel canister that engine exhaust is routed through to reduce emissions by means of a chemical reaction. Like other exhaust parts, the converter may wear out and need replacement. It's important for you to remember that the catalytic converter is covered by the vehicle manufacturer's five year, 50,000 mile warranty. If you have a converter problem, and the car is still under warranty, see your new car dealer.

If you are about to replace the catalytic converter in the

exhaust system with a straight pipe with hopes of better performance, think twice. Anyone who tampers with a vehicle's exhaust and removes or replaces components with non-approved (CARB/EPA) components can be penalized $2,500 per vehicle or more. Besides that, "pulling" your converter doesn't improve performance on an emission-controlled vehicle; it can have the opposite effect.

## EXHAUST FUMES

Could your vehicle's trunk lid or rear tailgate be putting you to sleep? You may be getting exhaust gas fumes inside your car and not be aware of it until it's too late. Many cars, old and new, have a truck or rear tailgate rubber seal or molding that is worn out or doesn't fit properly. Usually the driver is not aware of this potentially *dangerous* condition.

As a result of air turbulence at the rear of a vehicle while at highway speed, exhaust gases will seep through a poorly sealed trunk or rear tailgate on a wagon-type vehicle and enter the passenger compartment. Before you know it, you're feeling drowsy, or you may even fall asleep at the wheel.

To check on these rubber seals, take a sheet of notebook paper, place it over the seal, and close the trunk or tailgate. Now try to pull out the paper; if it comes out easily you should make necessary adjustments or even replace the seals. Do this test along the entire molding surface at least once a year. It could save your life.

## PARTS

If you need to replace other parts, I recommend using original equipment replacement exhaust components if possible.

For pipes, mufflers, hangers, etc., the "factory" parts have always fit properly and performed correctly for me.

My advice is that you have the exhaust system checked at least every six months or at every major service. Remember, a properly operating exhaust system not only affects engine performance, but also assures the safety of everyone inside the vehicle.

# DRIVETRAIN

□ □ □

A vehicle's drivetrain includes the power-transmitting components of the vehicle: engine, clutch, transmission, driveshaft, U joints, differential, axles, and wheels. Most of us don't think much about our vehicle's drive train until something goes wrong: strange noises, leaks, or shifting problems. That's when we begin worrying about a big repair job. This chapter will include

- Drivetrain components
- Automatic transmission
- Automatic transmission fluid
- Automatic transmission repair
- Constant velocity (CV) joints

Is your car front wheel drive or rear wheel drive? Front wheel drive incorporates engine, transmission, and driving axle in one compact unit. Rear wheel drive delivers front engine power to the rear wheels through a transmission, driveshaft, and differential.

## DRIVETRAIN COMPONENTS

**Clutch or Torque Converter:** Clutch with manual transmission or torque converter with automatic permits smooth transfer of power from the engine to the transmission.

**Transaxle:** Combines transmission and driving axles in a

compact unit, saving weight and space inside the passenger compartment.

**CV (Constant Velocity) Joints:** Deliver power to the wheels, twisting and flexing like a wrist joint as the wheels turn and the suspension moves over bumps. They are packed with grease and covered with rubber boots.

**Transmission:** Whether front drive or rear, this is the gear-shifting mechanism that matches engine speed to road speed and load.

**Universal Joints:** Provide flexibility on a rear drive vehicle between the transmission and the rear axle, allowing the axle to move with the irregularities in the road.

**Driveshaft:** The tubular component connecting the transmission to the rear axle.

**Differential:** The round housing at the center of the rear axle. It directs power to the driving wheels and, through its gearing mechanism, permits wheels to turn at different speeds in turns.

## AUTOMATIC TRANSMISSION

How can you keep from spending big money on transmission repairs?

First, it's important to include automatic transmission fluid changes as part of your maintenance program (see your owner's manual). To point out how important this is, let's look at how an automatic transmission works:

Everything in an automatic transmission works hydraulically. No gears actually change as in a standard shift transmission; it is all done through hydraulic pressure. Automatic transmission fluid is probably the most complex of all the lubricants your car needs. As the fluid gets old, it picks up lots of foreign objects from inside your transmission and will start to break down, eventually leading to deterioration in transmission parts. The internal seals of the transmission will be the first to go. Clean and fresh fluid keeps your seals soft and pliable.

Automatic transmission fluid performs three functions: It acts as a lubricant between gears and sliding elements within the transmission, it serves as the transmission's cooling medium, and it delivers hydraulic pressure.

Automatic transmission fluid also has a detergent in it, to keep the transmission clean, and is resistant to the higher temperatures common in automatic transmissions.

## CHECKING AND CHANGING
### TRANSMISSION FLUID

I recommend changing the transmission fluid, with normal driving, every 30,000 miles or every two to three years (see owner's manual). If you regularly use your vehicle to tow a trailer or for any other severe use, change your fluid every 10,000 to 20,000 miles. For RV owners, I suggest changing the fluid every year. (During hot weather driving, remember that the automatic transmission fluid is cooled by the engine cooling system (radiator) on most cars.)

### FOR MANUAL TRANSMISSIONS

1. Check the fluid level by removing the filler plug, which is located on the side of the transmission case (you usually have to get under the car to reach the filler plug).
2. The oil level is considered sufficient if you can wet your finger without having to bend more than your first knuckle.

### FOR AUTOMATIC TRANSMISSIONS

1. Check fluid monthly with the engine fully warm, idling in park or neutral, with the brake set.
2. The fluid is checked with a dipstick, as with engine oil.

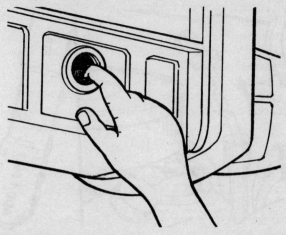

*Checking manual transmission fluid*
*Art by Tim Kreger*

If the fluid level is low, fill with the correct type of fluid for your car (check owner's manual). A brownish, gritty, or burned-smelling fluid is a sign of trouble. Changing transmission fluid and filter at recommended intervals will help prevent transmission damage.

A new transmission fluid debuted recently called Dexron III, with claims that no changing is necessary as long as the vehicle is used in normal conditions. It may work fine if your driving habits include very little stop-and-go driving (mostly interstate).

## AUTOMATIC TRANSMISSION REPAIR

If a technician determines that the transmission is due for a major repair, follow this guideline before you authorize the work: Make sure that the problem is definitely with the transmission and not from other components. This may sound elementary; however, noise that sounds like it's com-

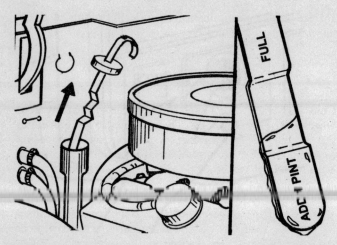

*Checking automatic transmission fluid*          *Art by Tim Kreger*

ing from the transmission may actually be from the tires, U-joints, driveshaft, or differential. Poor shifting may even be a result of an engine problem.

Remember, about 90 percent of transmission failures are due to the neglect of changing fluid at proper intervals.

Tips for long and prosperous relationship between you and your car's automatic transmission:

- After starting the engine, allow idle speed to slow to normal before shifting.
- Avoid holding one foot on the brake, the other on the accelerator.
- Never rock your car more than a few times when stuck in snow. Rocking overheats the transmission.
- Check transmission fluid every 30 days.
- If you need to add fluid, check for leakage.

**Note:** If you are a "severe service" driver (trailer towing or other abnormal loads), check your owner's manual for special service requirements. Consider installing an auxiliary transmission cooler.

## CV JOINTS

Constant Velocity (CV) joints are a primary part of any front wheel drive (FWD) vehicle. They provide power transfer to the wheels, while allowing for steering and suspension movement. CV joints are designed to maintain a constant shaft speed, regardless of operating speed and angle, without vibration.

They're located between the transaxle (that's the term for a front wheel drive transmission) and the wheels, and they have to flex up and down on a bumpy road, and sideways as the wheels steer. They're protected by rubber boots filled with lubricant.

CV joints are pretty rugged and will generally go at least 100,000 miles without requiring replacement. The main reason why they fail prematurely is lack of lubrication due to a worn-out (torn) rubber boot attached over the CV joint.

If a damaged boot should allow lubricant to leak out, that hardworking CV joint quickly could and will self-destruct. In my opinion, this is a major drawback with the design of the common transaxle in front wheel drive vehicles. I recommend frequent inspection of these protective boots for

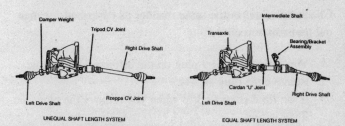

*Typical front wheel drive systems*
*Perfect Circle-Dana Corporation. Used by permission*

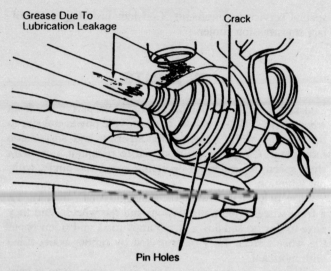

*Checking CV joint boot*
*Perfect Circle-Dana Corporation. Used with permission.*

signs of boot damage or leaks. This should be every three to four months or 3,000 to 4,000 miles.

## DIFFERENTIAL OIL

Check this fluid in the same manner as described for manual transmission oil.

1. You'll find the filler plug on the differential housing.
2. Remove the plug slowly.
3. If the fluid starts to drip when you remove the plug, the level is fine.
4. If fluid level is low, you'll need to seek a technician to add fluid since it needs to be professionally pumped in.

# MOTORING TIP

## TRAILER TOWING

When it looks like you'll be able to enjoy some nice weather, you may be planning to hook up your trailer or boat and hit the road for a weekend getaway.

However, it's important that you realize that towing is serious business and that you'll find trouble if you're not familiar with the proper technique and precautions.

First you need to know how much your vehicle can and should tow. A lot of times people are quite disappointed when they find out that they can't pull their trailer or boat up a steep grade. You've probably seen those motorists going uphill in the far right lane at 15 to 20 miles per hour (or you may even have been one of those folks).

I believe this to be the most misunderstood aspect of towing—many people just do not know what trouble they can get into when they tow "over limit" for their particular vehicle. They could lose a trailer, damage the engine, or cause a serious accident.

Automakers supply towing ratings in their new vehicle literature and the owner's manual. You can also pick up a copy of the highly respected monthly magazine on trailering, *Trailer Life*. I know that they publish a tow vehicle issue every spring.

I would always insist on the towing package option when purchasing a new vehicle. The vehicle will last longer and have a higher resale value.

When deciding on a travel trailer, try to determine the trailer's "loaded weight." This means when the gas tanks are full and all of your gear is on board. You may find out that this weight is considerably higher than the trailer's published weight. This extra hundred or so pounds could make your tow very difficult, even hazardous, if you're at or over your vehicle's towing limit.

Now that you have determined how much you can safely tow, let's hitch you up.

There are four classes of hitches: Class I for trailers up to 2,000 pounds, Class II for trailers up to 3,500 pounds, Class III for trailers up to 5,000 pounds, and Class IV for trailers between 5,000 and 10,000 pounds.

There are important installation factors and on-the-road adjustments to your hitch that are critical for safety. Make sure your hitch is installed by an experienced RV service center. Your installer will also provide you with adjustment procedures.

Now that you're on the road, here are some safety tips:

- Keep your speed down. Don't exceed 55 miles per hour. Your stopping distances are considerably longer because of the additional weight, so allow extra space between you and the car ahead of you.
- Have extra-wide mirrors installed at your RV service facility, and use them. This is the only way to see what's behind you. (Some light trucks, such as the GM Suburban and Ford Expedition have factory mirrors already designed for towing.)
- Make sure your safety chains are in place before you leave.
- Have someone outside of your vehicle check your trailer's running and brake lights.
- While traveling, use only the right lane at all times (except when passing another vehicle), and always be thinking ahead. Don't catch yourself daydreaming about your destination, because towing is very serious business and requires concentration.

I hope my tips on towing were helpful. Have a good time, and remember: Don't overload yourself!

# THE BRAKING SYSTEM

❑ ❑ ❑

Even more important than keeping a car on the go is getting it to stop—on command. From a safety standpoint, the brake system is the most important system on your car. As a result, brake failure is the number one fear among drivers. This chapter covers:

- How your brakes work
- Brake system components
- Common braking problems
- Brake system inspection
- Brake fluid changing
- Resurfacing brake rotors/discs

If your reaction time is typical, you'll travel about seventy feet in an emergency stop from 65 mph before your foot reaches the brake pedal. With visual problems, such as poor eyesight, bad lights, or windshield wipers, or if you're experiencing the effects of medicine or alcohol, reaction time will be slower.

Further, if you've neglected mechanical maintenance, hitting the brake pedal may be only the beginning of your crisis. Erratic braking action can cause a bad emergency situation to become worse, as it can pull your car right into the accident—or the car may not stop at all.

Despite recent advancements in braking system design, including antilock brakes (ABS), this vital safety system is among the most neglected on our motor vehicles and a leading mechanical cause of accidents.

The chain of events that occur in your car's braking system is, as the expression goes, as strong as its weakest link. A malfunction of any part of the system can cause brakes to be erratic or to fail completely.

All components of the braking system do not wear out or malfunction at the same time, although it may seem that way. You could drive for thousands of miles and never experience a bit of trouble with your brakes. Then all of a sudden, you attempt a sudden stop and your brakes fail. If you drive normally and do not abuse your brakes, it's still possible to have a dangerous brake condition and not realize it.

# HYDRAULIC BRAKING SYSTEM PRINCIPLES

## HOW THE BRAKING SYSTEM WORKS

The brake pedal pushes on the master cylinder's piston(s) to create hydraulic pressure. This pressure is transmitted through steel tubes and flexible hoses. Cylinders and pistons at the wheels receive this pressure and convert it into mechanical force to press friction material against the drums or rotors. The greater the brake pedal force, the harder the friction material is pressed against the drum or rotor. This way, the driver can control braking by varying pedal pressure as driving conditions dictate.

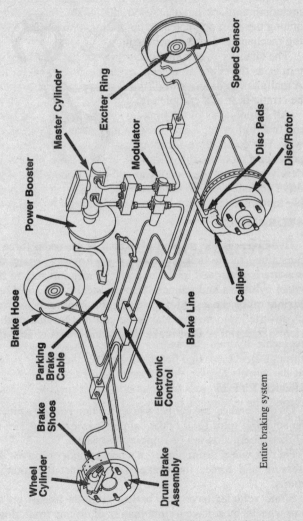

Speed Sensor

Exciter Ring

Master Cylinder

Modulator

Power Booster

Disc Pads

Disc/Rotor

Caliper

Brake Hose

Parking
Brake
Cable

Brake Line

Electronic
Control

Brake
Shoes

Wheel
Cylinder

Drum Brake
Assembly

Entire braking system

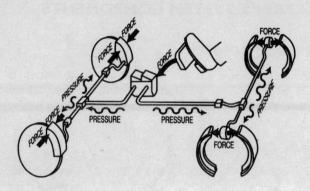

Wagner Brake Products. Used with permission.

## HYDRAULICS

Hydraulics is the method by which brake pedal force is transmitted to the brakes located at each wheel. Hydraulic pressure is generated in the master cylinder and sent to the wheel cylinders and calipers through steel brake lines and flexible rubber hoses. At the wheels, this hydraulic pressure is converted into mechanical force and motion that pushes friction material against brake drums and rotors to stop the vehicle.

## BRAKE TYPES

On disc brakes, the caliper causes friction pads to squeeze the spinning rotor (like brake calipers squeezing the rim of a bike wheel), slowing or stopping the wheel.

On rear wheel drum brakes, a wheel cylinder receives the pressure and forces the brake shoes against the rotating drums.

Some vehicles have disc brakes or drum brakes on all four wheels; most have a combination of disc on front, drum on rear. In every case it is friction that stops the vehicle.

# BRAKE SYSTEM COMPONENTS

## MASTER CYLINDERS

The master cylinder is the "heart" of any brake system. It stores brake fluid and generates hydraulic pressure. There are several master cylinder types to meet application needs.

## BRAKE CHEMICALS

Brake fluid is the brake system's "blood." There are different grades to meet brake system operating conditions and temperatures. The most commonly used brake fluid is DOT 3. Refer to your owner's manual for your specific type of brake fluid. Other fluids include DOT 4, DOT 5, and silicone fluid.

## POWER BOOSTERS

Power boosters work with the brake pedal and master cylinder to increase hydraulic force and make stopping easier. There are several power booster types, each using a different power source.

## VALVES

Brake systems have pressure regulating valves. They control hydraulic pressure application to the front and rear brakes under different stopping conditions.

## LINES AND HOSES

Steel brake lines and flexible rubber hoses are the brake system's "arteries." They transmit hydraulic pressure from the master cylinder to the wheels.

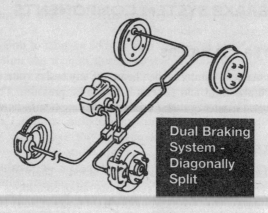

*Wagner Brake Products. Used with permission.*

## SPLIT SYSTEMS

Split systems divide the hydraulic system into two circuits. In case of a failure in one, the other circuit remains operable to provide limited brake operation.

## ABS COMPONENTS

ABS (antilock brake system) is a feature on many late-model vehicles. ABS improves vehicle braking by preventing wheel lockup during panic stops.

## COMMON BRAKE PROBLEM SYMPTOMS

**Vehicle Pulls** to one side when brakes are applied. A tire may be underinflated, or brakes misadjusted or in need of repair.

**Squealing or Grinding Noises, or Unreliable Stopping** can be signs of worn pads or shoe linings. If the pads or linings are worn too badly, they can score drums or rotors, greatly reducing braking efficiency.

**Brake Noise or Squeal** may also be a signal of dragging brake shoes or pads, which can result in poor gas mileage, premature wear of linings, and damage to drum or rotor friction surfaces.

**Brake Chatter and Pedal Pulsation** can indicate a warped or out-of-round rotor or brake drum surface. Excessive pedal travel, or "bottoming out" of pedal, may even mean the drum or rotor is out of safe limits.

**Unreliable and Inconsistent Stopping or Grabbing Brakes** are often signs of a leaking caliper, master cylinder, or wheel cylinder. If undetected too long, this situation can cause partial system failure.

**A Soft Pedal, or Excessive Pedal Effort** can be an indication of several problems, including a leak in the hydraulic system or low fluid level.

**Excessive Pad Wear** can be the result of installation of the wrong-quality grade for the type of driving you do. If you tow a vehicle, haul weight consistently, live in a hilly or mountainous terrain, or perform quick or sudden stops from either low or high speeds, you probably should be installing a premium pad or brake shoe.

Total brake system performance relies on all components operating properly. All components wear and deteriorate with use and age. When one component requires service or replacement, chances are other components will, too. Additionally, a failure in one area of the system may display a symptom in another. It's vitally important to always think of brakes as a "system." Due to the nature of failure symptoms, causes may not be associated with the identified components. Only accurate diagnosis of the entire system can isolate the exact causes.

Be aware of these warning signs. And as soon as any one of them occurs, take your car to a professional technician for an inspection. He will be able to explain what brake services your car may need, and make any necessary repairs.

# INSPECTING YOUR BRAKES

Brake inspections are one of life's little details that car owners should do without fail. It should be taken care of at least every six months, like getting a physical.

With most braking systems having over 150 different parts, not to mention the advent of computerized antilock systems, most of us should leave this job to the well-equipped professional. If faced with the "good, better, best" option, consider that there's no room for anything less than the best in brake work. Always insist on quality parts from a reputable source.

A brake inspection should include the following components:

**Master Cylinder:** It is located on most cars on the firewall and should be checked periodically to ensure the proper fluid level.

**Brake Lines:** Brake lines should be inspected for rust, which can lead to leaks. If the lines are damaged, they should be replaced.

**Brake Hoses:** Rubber brake hoses run from the brake lines to the brake calipers and wheel cylinders. Constant exposure to road grime, dirt, salt, and other elements can cause the rubber to become brittle and crack, leading to brake failure.

**Lining and Pads:** The pads and brake shoe linings should be checked periodically for uneven or excessive wear, glazing, or saturation from brake fluid or grease.

**Calipers and Wheel Cylinders:** Brakes are activated by brake fluid pressure from the master cylinder, which pushes a piston located in the caliper or wheel cylinder against the pad or shoe. A leak here can cause erratic braking or brake failure.

**Bearings and Seals:** Wheel bearings should be inspected and lubricated periodically. Worn wheel bearings, which can cause faulty steering as well as erratic braking, should be replaced.

**Parking Brake:** The parking brake should be adjusted periodically.

**Wheels and Tires:** The insides of the wheels and tires should also be checked for any trace of brake fluid. If you see any fluid on either of these two surfaces, you're probably leaking brake fluid and should have it repaired immediately.

## CHANGING BRAKE FLUID

Even though the braking system is closed/sealed, moisture can be absorbed through the system's rubber components (hoses, seals, cups, etc.). Brake system problems can begin when brake fluid has a moisture content of as little as 3 percent.

- 3 percent moisture content can lower brake fluid's boiling point by as much as 30 percent.
- 3 percent moisture content renders the anticorrosion additives ineffective.

**3 percent moisture content can take place in as little as eight months to one year, depending on atmospheric and other conditions (as living in wet, high humidity climates).**

Brake fluid reaches its saturation point at 7 percent moisture content. After that, moisture can no longer be absorbed and becomes water droplets. It is not unusual for a vehicle's brake fluid to reach this saturation point after only a few years of service.

Airborne moisture also enters the system every time the master cylinder reservoir is opened to check the brake fluid level. That's why you should *never* remove the cap to do this chore: The reservoirs are "see-through" for just this reason!

On some older cars, **you will** have to remove the cap!

- The higher the moisture content, the more likely the brake fluid is to boil. Brake fluid boil can lead to steam in the system. Steam is a gas, and thus is not compressible. This can lead to a spongy, soft pedal.
- The higher the moisture content, the more susceptible the brake fluid is to freezing. Ice crystals can form in the system, impeding brake fluid movement, which can lead to system failure.
- The higher the moisture content, the lower the corrosion-resistant properties of the brake fluid. This can lead to internal rust and deterioration, resulting in premature wear and/or component failure.

**Brake fluid should be flushed and replaced every two years or 20,000 miles,** and should become a part of your vehicle's normal periodic maintenance. It is cheap insurance against internal corrosion, pedal loss due to brake fluid boil, and/or complete braking failure.

## TURNING BRAKE ROTORS/DISCS

Now, this is an important tip for owners of front wheel drive vehicles. If you're in for a *complete* brake job, make sure that if your front brake rotors or discs require resurfacing, it's done *on* the car, with the use of an on-vehicle brake lathe (a piece of equipment that actually is attached to a wheel to perform brake disc resurfacing).

Most shops have equipment that "turns" or resurfaces brake discs (rotors) when you have a major brake job done. This is done to eliminate the "shake" when discs are warped due to heat after miles of wear, and any damage to the rotors from a worn-out pad.

What's important for you to insist on when you get a brake job is that the brake discs are "turned" or resurfaced *while they are still on the car* if you have a front wheel drive car. This is so you match the brake discs to the car, not to a machine that's elsewhere.

I've seen rotors that have been turned off the car and then put back on the car, and there is still a vibration when a foot steps on the brake. When the technician turns the discs on the car, the brake machine takes into account the looseness common in the front wheel bearings and hubs on many front wheel drive cars.

If you drive a front wheel drive car, be sure to ask how your front discs are turned if you're looking to have a major brake job done. (If it were my vehicle, front wheel drive *or* rear drive, I would always have the rotors turned on the vehicle; it's just a better job!)

Think of your car's brake system as an extension of your body. If you push on the pedal and the car doesn't respond as you expect it to, you may be in trouble. When your brakes feel good, you'll feel better about driving. There are no shortcuts on brake work. Invest in the best service you can get.

# THE SUSPENSION AND STEERING SYSTEM

□ □ □

A common cause of highway accidents is the driver's loss of control of the vehicle. Reasons vary, including driving too fast for conditions, rough road surface, momentary inattention at the wheel, and many more, but the net result is an accident. In this chapter you'll find

- Checking suspension and steering
- How shocks and struts affect performance
- When to replace shocks and struts

In many cases a more "forgiving" car can help avoid such a crisis. The term refers to a car's ability to cling to the road when the driver enters a curve too fast, or stay on course when the wheels run onto the shoulder of the road.

A valuable safety feature of a late-model car is its excellent handling characteristics. Good roadability, which can help keep you out of trouble, should remain yours for the life of your car *if* you practice preventive maintenance. This means regular checks, service, and replacement of critical systems like the suspension and suspension system.

For the average car owner, the suspension system on an automobile is out of sight and out of mind until a "clunking" noise, bumpy ride, or a loose (not in control) feeling gets his or her attention.

What's unknown to most drivers is that there is a good chance at least one of their vehicle's wheels is riding *below* its specified level. What that means to the car owner is the potential for road wander or a harsh, bumpy ride when carrying additional passengers or heavy loads, or when towing. What it could mean to the car is rapid and uneven wear on its tires, shocks, struts, springs, and other parts of the suspension system.

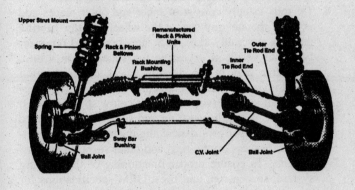

MacPherson strut suspension with rack and pinion steering
*Moog Automotive. Used with permission.*

# CHECKING SUSPENSION AND STEERING

1. The first and easiest thing to check is the air pressure of the tires with a tire pressure gauge. Pressure should always be set at the recommendation of the vehicle manufacturer. The pressure of the tires directly affects the

ride of the vehicle. Also, check the condition of the tires. A worn tire can affect handling, even if the vehicle is properly aligned. (See "Tires" chapter.)

2. Ball joints carry the weight of the front end and are the pivot points between the tires and the suspension. When a ball joint fails, erratic steering and premature tire wear, or even loosening of a wheel, are the most common results.

3. Bushings are expected to dampen road shock, support vehicle weight, control suspension movement, absorb braking forces, and suppress road noise. Worn bushings can create a steering pull, brake pull, or wheel shimmy at all speeds, and thus cause excessive tire wear.

4. Tie rods usually consist of inner and outer pieces and connect the steering arm at the wheel and the steering gearbox assembly (i.e., rack and pinion). Looseness here may result in excessive tire squealing in a turn, more free play in the steering wheel, or the steering wheel no longer being centered.

5. Worn-out springs (vehicle height below specifications) can force the entire steering and suspension system to go out of proper geometrical alignment, resulting in unnecessary wear on the tires and other suspension components. To ensure proper functioning of the steering system, suspension, and tires, OEM specifications for chassis height must be maintained. And proper chassis height depends on the springs. In the long run, improper chassis height can be unsafe and uneconomical, causing handling problems, robbing tires of maximum tread life, and increasing the loss of fuel economy.

Indications of worn springs start to show up around 30,000 plus miles. When a car comes in for an inspection, the technician should look at how the car sets: Is it down in front, or is it leaning to one side, or is the rear end too low? As the car is driven, the technician should observe how the vehicle reacts to braking and whether the steering wheel is straight.

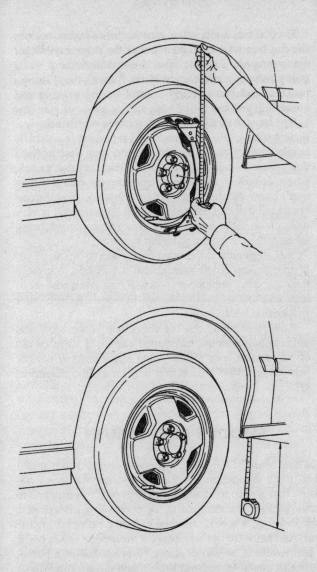

**Vehicle height measurement**   *Moog Automotive. Used with permission.*

Do you feel a jolt when your car hits a bump, or does the car drag when you back out of the driveway? Other symptoms are a severe up-and-down movement while going over a washboard surface, "nosediving" during braking, reduced steering control during braking and cornering, and excessive body roll or a loss of stability.

The most effective way to determine whether any vehicle's springs are weak and need replacing is a vehicle height inspection. A primary reason many technicians don't measure height more often is that they don't know where or how to measure different model cars and they don't know where to get that information. Manufacturers do publish that information, but sometimes it is very difficult to find. Insist upon this measurement being taken if these symptoms sound familiar.

6. Wheel alignment is the most likely area to be out of adjustment. And if left unadjusted, it will cost you more than any other component—it will cost you a new set of tires and loss of fuel economy, besides affecting other suspension components.

   And remember, any of the other suspension and steering components mentioned earlier, if worn or out of adjustment, can affect wheel alignment, so it's not just running into a curb that will knock the alignment off.

## SHOCKS AND STRUTS

In the true sense of the word, a *shock absorber* is not an absorber, it's a dampener. It's the springs, not the shock absorbers, that absorb road shocks. However, if a spring had to do this without the dampening or controlling effects of a shock absorber, it would continue to bounce after hitting the bump. And since the springs support the weight of the body, the entire vehicle would continue to bounce after a bump, creating an unstable, uncomfortable, and unsafe condition.

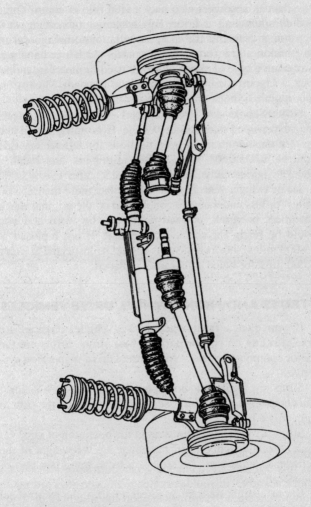

Typical front wheel drive components

*Moog Automotive. Used with permission.*

While dampening of spring action still is their main purpose, shock absorbers also play a vital role in controlling a vehicle's handling and ride. By dampening (absorbing) suspension movement, the lower oscillations (movement) of suspension allow for a smoother ride and better handling. Struts are a type of shock absorber used in most late model cars, a support member of a suspension system. Most struts incorporate a shock absorber and coil spring.

**Note:** Shocks and struts are part of the complex steering/suspension system of the vehicle. Everything within that system must conform to specifications for satisfactory ride control and safety. Have wheel alignment and balance checked periodically; inspect and rotate tires every 5,000 miles or twice a year. If your vehicle has more than 25,000 miles (or less under severe conditions) on the original shock absorbers or struts, internal parts may be worn and you could be ready for shock replacement. If not replaced at 25,000 miles, shocks and struts should be inspected at every 6,000 miles or twice a year until replaced.

## STRUTS AND FRONT WHEEL DRIVE VEHICLES

If you own a front wheel drive vehicle, chances are you're riding on two or perhaps four struts. Struts are the major component of most front wheel drive suspension systems.

Struts are similar to shock absorbers inside a "housing." This housing is part of an assembly that connects the strut to the vehicle body.

Struts are critically important in the operation of your vehicle. Struts actually assist in supporting the weight of the vehicle. In most cars, the strut is also an important part of the steering system.

Because struts are such an integral part of the front wheel drive suspension system, they are generally more expensive than shocks to replace.

It's important to note that strut suspensions take up less

room than coil spring and shock absorber set-ups (most struts combine shock and spring in one unit) and are ideal for fuel-efficient cars. This is because struts take the place of many other front-end components.

## RESULTS OF WORN STRUTS AND SHOCKS

Worn struts or shocks can increase wear of tires, ball joints, steering linkage, springs, or constant velocity (CV) joints.

Good vehicle maintenance can eliminate wear and tear on undercar parts and your wallet. A vehicle with worn shock absorbers or struts is more vulnerable to undercarriage damage. One severe jolt from a pothole, for example, can damage exhaust system brackets, transmission pan, radiator mounts, or other parts.

On a rough, winding road, the driver of a car with worn shocks/struts is in danger of losing control. Weak shocks or struts permit excessive rebound of the wheels, allowing them to become airborne. During this brief period the tire loses contact with the road surface. All steering, braking, and handling is lost.

Shock absorbers and struts seldom go bad all at once. Instead, they gradually lose their ability to control the vehicle's stability. You may be unaware of deteriorating ride control until the condition has become serious. For this reason it's wise to test and inspect shocks and struts regularly. (Every time your car is serviced).

## SHOCK/STRUT INSPECTION

Oil residue on the outside of a shock absorber indicates a leak. To check the shocks, bounce the car several times at each corner, one corner at a time (by pushing down on the fender). If the car bounces more than twice after you let go, the shock absorber/strut needs replacement.

If the shock absorbers/struts pass this test, wipe them

clean of fluid and check again in two or three days. If oil residue reappears, change the shocks. Shock absorbers/ struts do not have to be changed all at once, but should be changed in pairs by front and rear.

## GAS-CHARGED SHOCKS AND STRUTS

As far as replacing shocks or struts, I suggest a good-quality gas unit. Gas-filled shocks/struts are better for year-round driving since they are not affected by differences in temperature, as fluid-filled shock absorbers are. Other gas shock/strut advantages include

- *Improved roll stability,* which decreases the tendency of a vehicle to sway from side to side when turning a corner or a sharp curve. Gas charging reduces roll.
- *Reduced noise.* Much of your vehicle's interior noise comes from excessive road vibration. Because gas-charged shocks and struts reduce vibration, they also help reduce the noise level in your car or truck.
- *Reduced harsh ride,* which results when tires transfer vibration from road imperfections to the passenger compartment, causing an uncomfortable ride or even loss of control. Gas-charged shocks and struts control tire motion better, so you feel the roughness of the road less.
- *Consistent performance.* During prolonged use, shocks can lose their ability to absorb vibration because as they heat up, fluid inside the reserve tube begins to foam. The gas charge virtually eliminates the aeration or foaming that occurs in a standard shock. This means more consistent performance over a wider range of driving conditions.
- *Improved stability,* a boost in spring-absorbing capacity that cannot be found in standard products.
- *Better handling and a smoother, safer ride,* because the gas charge allows ride engineers to fine-tune the

valving in shocks or struts. This means you get more comfort at low-speed conditions without sacrificing the control required at high speeds. This accuracy in valving is difficult to achieve in a non-gas shock.

It certainly makes sense to have your shocks and struts inspected whenever your car is in for service.

# MOTORING TIP

## SPOTS ON THE GARAGE FLOOR

Is your automobile trying to communicate with you?

Look at what's on the ground underneath it. Those leaks or drips may be a sign of trouble.

Let's look at the colors of the vital fluids that your car may be leaking.

**Black or Dark Brown:** Most likely engine oil. Small drops over a period of time are not unusual. If you see moderate-sized puddles, have your technician check out the car for a leak.

**Bright Green or Bright Yellow:** Radiator coolant/antifreeze. If you spot a moderate amount under your car, check the radiator level by looking in the radiator after *carefully* removing the cap **(when your engine is cold)**. You should not be looking at the overflow tank, only in the radiator.

**Rusty or Orange:** Probably coolant, with rusty water mixed into your cooling system. See a professional, have your system flushed, and add new coolant/antifreeze. (This should be done every two to three years anyway.)

**Red or Pink Fluid:** Most likely from the automatic transmission. A small drop is really nothing to worry about, but since transmission repairs tend to be expensive, keep an eye on your fluid level, and add when necessary (do not over-fill).

**Red, Pink, or Clear Fluid:** If oily to the touch and (in most cases) found on the driver's side, toward the front bumper, it's probably power steering fluid. Add fluid as needed. Some power steering fluid is clear and some brake fluids are clear. To tell the difference, put a little on your finger and add water—power steering fluid will remain oily and won't wash away. If you're in doubt, get a professional to determine if the fluid is leaking from power steering or brake components.

Here's a tip on checking the color of what's leaking: Don't use newspaper or any paper material because it will absorb the fluid, thereby changing its color. My wife Dixie Bell takes a roll of tinfoil and spreads it out under the car to catch the drips. Then she is able to see the actual color and show the technician.

**Remember,** a leak can be critical. A faulty gasket or seal, usually an inexpensive "fix," can end up costing a mint if it's not taken care of.

☐ ☐ ☐

# THE AUTOMOTIVE EXPERIENCE

# BUYING A CAR

□ □ □

If you are in the market for a new car, I'll bet that most of you are not looking forward to going through the negotiations that the car buying process has been known for.

You'll be pleasantly surprised once you set foot in a new car dealership, with the change in the attitude the dealers now have toward customers. This may even be a big shock, especially if you have not been shopping for a new car in the last five years.

I must say, though, that some of the credit for this new customer-oriented attitude by dealers has to be given to my good friend Mr. J.D. Power and his Sales Satisfaction Index (SSI), which rates the entire dealer experience. The SSI rates new car dealers on their sales approach, delivery, and vehicle quality, and this index is published yearly for every new-model-year group of car makes.

OK, let's get into my tips on how to improve your chances of having an enjoyable experience while shopping for a new car:

- Before you go into a new car dealership, I would suggest you see a rental car agency. Some folks tell me after they buy a new car that it is not what they expected. Then I asked if they test drove the car. They say they did but were too nervous to really feel and evaluate the car they were planning to buy. It's an excellent idea to first rent the car or cars you're considering owning. You'll be able to use the car over a weekend or so and really decide if it's what you'll be happy in. No salesperson will be pressuring you.

- By really knowing what you want ahead of time, you'll also streamline your shopping time considerably. The salesperson will be more responsive to you as well.

- Discuss financing with your bank or credit union prior to visiting the car dealership. In most cases you'll still find that the manufacturers are offering the lowest finance rates. (If you already know that you'll be using dealer financing, bring your credit information into the dealership with you.)

- I wouldn't talk trade-in when shopping for a new car. Although it is more work, you can almost always do better by selling your car yourself. For its value, check the Blue Book, which can be found at most banks or libraries.

- Don't get too deep into a deal with a dealer until you've settled upon a certain model they have *in stock.* You'll get your best price on a car they have on hand. The longer a car sits in their inventory, the more money the dealership has paid to the bank on "flooring" it. So they would like to see it move out of their inventory and into someone's garage.

- When you're visiting a dealership, only bring with you those involved in the buying decision. If your kids have a say, as in backseat room in a minivan, bring them along also. If not, leave them at home, along with all others who are not involved in the actual transaction. This will help you focus on the business at hand.

- Here is an alternative for those of you who are experiencing sticker shock this year: "program" cars. These almost new vehicles are ones that rental agencies offer to dealers when they have been in the rental fleet for about six months. (They could also be cars out of the manufacturer's executive demo fleet.) These cars usually are current-year models. They have around 5,000 to 10,000 miles on the odometer and carry the new vehicle warranty. I've known of some cases where these program cars sold for more than one-third off the original sticker price! If one of these cars interests you, call local new car dealers and ask if they have program cars available.

## BEING A CAR-SAVVY BUYER

How many times have you read automotive literature or an ad and not had any idea what those technical terms meant? Have you ever walked into an auto agency and had a salesperson describe all of those advanced features you might need or enjoy on your new car without having any idea what he's talking about?

Unfortunately, a lot of automakers and salespeople alike just tell you the feature (e.g., active suspension) without explaining the benefit you'll receive from that feature. So, before you go shopping, check my glossary at the end of the book.

## TIPS WHEN SHOPPING FOR A USED CAR

- Shop during the day, not at night, when lights can hide flaws.
- Look for rust on the lower part of the car. Rust keeps spreading and is very expensive to repair.
- Examine the paint. If there's a new paint job, find out why. In general, stay away from used cars with new paint jobs. They could be hiding some real problems. A tip-off is if there's paint on the chrome or rubber trim.

- Take a magnet and move it around the car and fenders. If it sticks, fine. If not, the car may have been in an accident and poorly repaired with plastic filler (Except for fiberglass bodied cars like the Corvette or "kit" cars.).
- Stick your finger inside the tailpipe. If the powder is white or gray, it's okay. Black and gummy means there could be a big problem with the engine.
- Don't kick the tires. This only happens in the movies. But check them out by standing twenty feet behind. The tires should line up. And don't be wary about old tires; they can tell you a lot about alignment.
- Look at the gas cap. If the filler neck looks as though it's been widened, it might have been altered so the car can run on leaded fuel, thus damaging emission control equipment.
- Study the seats. Excessive wear shows a lot of use. If the backseats aren't worn, this was probably a one- or two-person car.
- Use your nose. A musty or overdeodorized smell might mean the car was once under water.
- Check the odometer. The average person drives approximately 10,000–12,000 miles a year. If the odometer reads too low, try to find out why. Don't give up if it's too high. Highway driving is better than town driving. On the highway the oil is allowed to reach the correct temperature and components will last longer. In town, during short errands, oil never gets to the correct operating temperature before the car is turned off. It all has to do with the length of time a vehicle is operating prior to shut down. In other words, a car from the "little old lady" might not be the best buy or best car.
- Check the service stickers on the door. They tell you how the car was maintained and could also prove the odometer mileage.
- Take the car for a test drive. If you're not allowed to do this, don't even think of buying the car. Check the

brakes, steering, heater, air conditioner. Listen to the engine with the radio off and the window rolled down.

• Then take the car to your favorite mechanic and have him check it over. He might find things like a safety defect in the windshield. He'll look under the hood and inside the engine. He can recognize inner body damage, bad hoses, leaky gaskets, etc., by raising the car on his service lift.

Here are a few more points on private party car shopping from the State Department of Motor Vehicles:

• Swindlers often try to sell more than one car. If you're responding to an ad, don't ask about a certain model. You should say, "Is the vehicle advertised still for sale?" Be careful if someone answers, "Which one?"

• Beware of people who sell cars in the street or in parking lots. Know the seller's true residence.

• Don't buy from someone who doesn't have the title or pink slip in their possession and own name. Check this paper over carefully for alterations or a note about the car being a "salvage" vehicle.

• Ask about the car's maintenance (records) and when and where the car was purchased. Be careful if the seller is hesitant.

# FINDING A GOOD TECHNICIAN

□ □ □

In light of recent news headlines, you may be wondering just whom you can trust to work on your vehicle. Don't despair, there are quite a few excellent repair facilities in your area. However, you need to follow my tips on finding one of those good shops and being treated fairly. My tips on selecting someone to service your automobile follow:

- The first and probably the most important tip is to ask for recommendations from family, friends, neighbors, or coworkers. When you are asking someone about the service they received on their automobile, also ask these three questions (which cover the most common complaints regarding automobile service):

  1. Did the person ever pay a higher price than originally quoted and, if so, why?
  2. Was the car ready at the time promised?
  3. Was it as clean as when the owner brought it in for service?

- After you've been given the name of a shop, call the Better Business Bureau, Chamber of Commerce, or other consumer affairs agency to check on the shop's reputation. Unfortunately a lot of people don't report a dishonest establishment to an agency of this type; they just look for someone else to service their automobile. So you may not get a list of shops to stay away from if you call, say, the Better Business Bureau. However, if you do get the name of a shop that has had complaints, you certainly should "steer clear."

- If you're on the road and your car needs to be serviced in an unfamiliar locale, you can still ask for recommendations. For instance, look for that one local café that's been around for years, have lunch or dinner there, and ask the owner or waitress. They are likely to direct you to the garage that works on all the local cars and trucks, instead of the service station adjacent to the highway.

- Once you've got the name of a shop you'd like to get service from, drive over and take a look. Is it neat and well organized? Appearance can sometimes offer a clue to how the business is run. A well-kept shop is a sign of pride in workmanship, and a place you will probably be happy with. Take a look at their equipment. To work on today's cars and trucks, you have to keep current with automotive technology. Besides the training technicians must go through, today's shop must have the latest computerized diagnostic equipment

- It's also a good sign if the facility you're considering displays emblems indicating they are AAA (American Automobile Association) or ASE (Automotive Service Excellence Institute) approved. These two organizations evaluate the qualifications of automotive technicians and repair facilities.

- Now that you've found a repair facility that looks good from the outside, drive on in and make an appointment for something simple like an oil change. By having something simple done, you'll usually find out whether you have made the right decision. If it's not the right place, you're not out a lot of money.

- Watch out for technicians who use scare tactics, saying you could get into an accident if you don't have this or that work done. While this could be a legitimate warning, it's also true that technicians have been known to take advantage of customers in this way.

- Always ask for an estimate, and get a copy of it before work begins. In most states, the technician has to get verbal or written authorization to proceed with any work not included on that estimate.
- If you're the type of person who likes to have old parts returned to them, be sure to tell the service writer when your order is being written up, not after the job is done. (Keep old hoses and belts in your trunk in case of an emergency).
- For major work, such as transmissions or engine rebuilds, I would suggest that you get at least two written estimates for the work. And make sure that the major work is really necessary by asking for another opinion.
- Have the technician list on the invoice any other faults he claims to find. No honest person will flinch at doing this—it's in his favor to have it in writing that he alerted you to the problems and that you declined to have them fixed.
- Make sure the price of the work is on the invoice.
- Considering all of the above technician/garage concerns, maybe the most important indicator of the character and expertise of the person to work on your vehicle is the car they drive. If it's a clean, sweet-running machine and a few years old, the technician may be the "car nut" that takes the most pride working on cars.

## FLAT RATE VS. HOURLY RATE

NOW, how about one of the most misunderstood areas in auto repair: the way most repair facilities charge for your service—the flat rate. Is it fair or should you be charged an hourly rate for service?

The flat rate is the number of hours a particular job (such as brakes) should take a "proficient" technician to do. These rates are published in repair guides by the auto manufacturer or independent publishers. If a three-hour job is performed in two hours, you'll be charged for three hours. Now, let me explain how a person working on your car can beat the flat rate.

Flat rate is based upon a technician using hand tools—not power tools—and working at average speed. However, if the technician working on your car has invested lots of money in power tools and is experienced, the flat rate time will normally be beaten. But should you look around town for someone who charges by the hour instead of the flat rate?

My best advice is to find a repair shop that is honest and dependable. Then you should stay with that shop and over the long run you'll find that your actual cost of repair will be lower and your level of satisfaction will be higher than if you shopped around for the best flat or hourly rate per job.

If you're happy with the shop, be sure to express your satisfaction with the technician, manager, and owner, if available. Let me tell you, a sincere thank-you from a customer goes a long, long way.

# GLOSSARY

## AUTOMOTIVE TERMS RELATING TO THE ENGINE AND DRIVETRAIN

**Overhead Cam vs Overhead Valve Engines:** The overhead valve engine (OHV) has been around a long time. The overhead cam engine (OHC) design is a relative newcomer to domestic automakers, although European and Asian automakers have used this design for a lot longer. The basic difference is that the lighter, critical valve train components of the overhead cam engine will let it speed up (rev) faster. An overhead valve (OHV) engine of the same displacement is more compact. Out in the real world, the OHV engine typically generates much more power (torque) at low-to-mid-range engine speeds. High-end (high-speed) power would be the best term to describe what you feel from an OHC engine.

**Compression Ratio:** Compression ratio is nothing more than the amount of pressure applied to the air/fuel mixture in the combustion chamber (above the engine's cylinder). The more air and fuel you can compress, the more power the engine produces. But there is a trade-off: Higher compression means higher octane, so premium fuel is required.

**Electronic Ignition System:** An ignition system wherein high voltage is sent to the spark plugs by electronic means, eliminating the need for replacing points and condenser. This system controls ignition and timing better and extends the life of the spark plugs. Tune-ups are needed less frequently. With electronic ignition, you'll have better fuel economy and more power, and you'll pollute the air less.

**Fuel Injection versus Carburetion:** Fuel injection is quite popular on all cars today. This is a fuel system that employs a mechanical or electronic sensing device to deliver a specific amount of fuel to the combustion chamber, depending on engine requirements. Fuel injection allows for better fuel economy, acceleration, and longer engine life.

**Two-Valve- versus Four-Valve-Per-Cylinder Engines:** Multi-valve engines have recently become fashionable. How many times have you heard "four valves per cylinder" in ads? This refers to an engine that has two intake valves and two exhaust valves (they usually just have one valve each). The extra valves allow the engine to breathe better and will increase power without having to increase the engine size.

**Horsepower versus Torque:** Both are measures of an engine's power. Horsepower is the energy (power) necessary to lift 550 pounds one foot in one second. Torque, the force produced by the engine, is what you want most of if you're always loaded down, as when towing, since torque allows an engine to work harder and longer.

**Electronic Automatic Transmission:** This type of transmission electronically selects the gear to provide smoother upshifts and downshifts while driving under any conditions. An electronic transmission will also last longer.

**Traction Control:** A computer-controlled system that uses electronic sensors to detect spin on drive wheels and then slows down the engine speed to regain traction on slippery surfaces like snow or ice.

**Turbocharger:** A device that boosts engine power by forcing air back into the combustion cycle. It operates off the exhaust system that powers a turbine, which pumps air back into the engine. Save your money if a turbocharger is offered as an option, unless you plan to do heavy towing or have additional power needs.

**Supercharger:** This unit compresses the engine's intake air above atmospheric pressure by means of an air pump operated by a belt. Superchargers usually can provide a power boost much more quickly than a turbo.

# TERMS RELATING TO THE CHASSIS AND SUSPENSION PART OF THE AUTOMOBILE

**Active Suspension:** A sophisticated, computer-controlled system that moves the vehicle's wheels while you drive. It compensates for any irregularities in the road to keep the car level, even while going around corners. An expensive option, it is not really necessary in ordinary driving.

**Aerodynamic Drag:** The drag produced when an automobile is moving and displaces the air in its path. It is a force usually measured in pounds, and it increases in proportion to a vehicle's frontal area, its drag coefficient. The sleeker your vehicle, the lower the drag coefficient and the better fuel economy you'll receive.

**All Wheel Drive versus Four Wheel Drive:** Are they the same? All wheel drive is a system where the engine's power is sent to all four wheels at all times. It is usually computer controlled and is most common on passenger cars and minivans. Four wheel drive is more common in sport utilities (all-purpose vehicles) and trucks. It is a system that is usually driver controlled, not computer controlled, to provide maximum traction over rough or wet surfaces.

**Antilock Brakes:** Also known as ABS, this is a computer-controlled braking system that detects an impending wheel lockup during a panic stop. It reduces the braking force by pulsing (pumping) the brakes many times per second. This reduces the chance of a skid, and the driver keeps control of the car.

**Four-Wheel Independent Suspension:** A suspension system where each wheel moves independently over the road, giving you the most control while driving, especially over rough surfaces and around corners. A good feature to look for in a new car.

**MacPherson Strut:** A device used as a suspension shock-absorbing component, in which a coil spring is mounted around a shock absorber. Very common on the front suspensions of today's cars, it gives you the most control of any type of suspension units.

**Rack-and-Pinion Steering:** A steering system that consists of a gear in conjunction with a toothed bar, called a rack. This system provides the most precise steering feel, along with the best control. It's also a simple system from a technician's point of view, with very few moving parts. Most cars have this system today.

**Torque Steer:** This is an undesirable tendency for a vehicle to turn in a particular direction during hard acceleration. It is common with most front wheel drive cars. (Although, with some newer cars, engineers have claimed to eliminate most of the torque steer.)

# GENERAL TERMS

**EPA Fuel Economy:** Lab tests by the EPA (Environmental Protection Agency) were used to determine what fuel economy a vehicle would get in the real world and these mpg numbers are listed on the car's window sticker. The city fuel economy figure is based on a drive through "typical" urban traffic. The highway economy figure uses a higher speed, which averages 49.4 mph. Both tests are done in a lab!

# ABOUT THE AUTHOR

"Motorman" Leon Kaplan, one of the nation's premier automotive experts, has been active in the auto industry for more than three decades and many claim that his heart "pumps motor oil." His weekly nationally syndicated "Motorman" radio show, gives him a unique opportunity to hear about motorized vehicles and diagnose automotive problems. This popular call-in program covers not only repair, maintenance and purchase concerns of all type motor vehicles, but also aircraft, boats and basically anything else that's motorized. It is the longest-running show of its kind and has the greatest audience.

Leon Kaplan wrote "The Motorized World of Leon Kaplan," a popular column featured in Petersen's *Motor Trend* Magazine.

A graduate of Nashville Auto/Diesel College in Tennessee, Kaplan has received many technical awards. He was inducted into the Nashville Auto/Diesel College Hall of Fame in 1989 and the National Association of Trade Technical Schools Hall of Fame in 1991.

As an industry consultant, his expertise is in demand by the auto industry, automobile dealerships, insurance companies, and the legal profession to provide expert opinion and testimony regarding all types of motorized vehicles.

Kaplan is president of Lancer Automotive Service, Inc. He has been servicing vehicles on the same street in Los Angeles for more than thirty years.

In addition to automotive interests, Kaplan has been a professional pilot for more than twenty-five years, with experience in all type of aircraft.

His experience also includes drag and stock car racing, motorcycle racing, and offshore, water ski, and drag boat racing.

# PENGUIN PUTNAM

online

Your Internet gateway to a virtual
environment with hundreds of entertaining
and enlightening books from
Penguin Putnam Inc.

While you're there, get the latest buzz on
the best authors and books around—
Tom Clancy, Patricia Cornwell, W.E.B. Griffin,
Nora Roberts, William Gibson, Robin Cook,
Brian Jacques, Catherine Coulter,
Stephen King, Jacquelyn Mitchard,
and many more!

Penguin Putnam Online is located at
http://www.penguinputnam.com

# PENGUIN PUTNAM NEWS

Every month you'll get an inside look at our
upcoming books and new features on our site.
This is an ongoing effort to provide you
with the most interesting and up-to-date
information about our books and authors.

Subscribe to Penguin Putnam News at
http://www.penguinputnam.com/ClubPPI